Technical Graphics at Junior Certificate

Guide to Better Grades

Higher and Ordinary Level

Assessment Structure

Technical graphics is examined at Ordinary and Higher Level in the Junior Certificate.

The papers at both levels are divided into two sections for a total of 400 marks.

Section A (120 marks) Short questions	15 questions (Answer 10)
Section B (280 marks) Long questions	6 questions (Answer 4)

Section A

Questions are presented on A3 paper and some of them are already partially completed. All questions in this section carry 12 marks. Sketches are required for some of them and these are drawn freehand. Shading or colour is sometimes required on these questions.

Tip: The sheet should be fixed to the drawing board to ensure accuracy when completing this section.

Section B

Questions must be answered on the A2 paper provided. Each question in the section is worth 70 marks.

Advanced Preparation

Be familiar with the layout and structure of the examination paper. This is best achieved by answering past examination questions from this book.

- This will improve your grades.

- It enables you to apply what you have studied to examination questions.

- It will assist you in improving your time management for the examination.

- It helps to promote confidence in advance of the examination.

Drawing equipment

Candidates will save time and improve grades by having a good set of clean drawing equipment. This must include sharp 2H grade pencils, compass and setsquares.

Time Management in the Exam

Ordinary Level – 2 hours 30 minutes

Higher Level – 3 hours

It is very important to adhere strictly to the time allocation guidelines shown below to ensure that you have the opportunity to complete the required number of questions. A small overrun in a few questions may result in a major loss of marks.

Level	Section A	Section B
Higher Level	40 minutes (4 min. per question)	140 minutes (35 min. per question)
Ordinary Level	30 minutes (3 min. per question)	120 minutes (30 min. per question)

Examination paper content

Section A – Higher Level

Freehand sketching

Surface development

Orthographic projection

Perspective projec~~~

Area conversions

Rotations

Truncated solids

Auxiliary elevations

Sectioned solids

Tangential arcs

CAD Commands

Graphs

Student Study Essentials

Section B – Higher level

This section has become fairly predictable in recent years though minor changes are sometimes noted.

The following topics generally appear in this section:

- **Orthographic projection**

It usually includes a portion of a truncated cylinder. The true shape of a given surface on the solid must also be found.

Tip: Position the drawing carefully on the sheet and avoid spending more than 35 minutes on the question.

- **Rotated Surface**

The surface usually includes a circular section which appears as an ellipse on the rotated view. A geometrical construction is sometimes required to set up the question.

Tip: Read the question carefully because it varies slightly each year.

- **Isometric Projection**

This question may be solved by either constructing an isometric scale or setting up the axonometric axes. It always includes a circular section.

Tip: The isometric scale is generally quicker to complete and carries the same marks.

- **Surface development**

A truncated cylinder or cone frequently features in this question.

Tip: The surface development should be carefully positioned to enable direct projection from the given elevation or plan.

- **Transformations**

In this question a simple shape is subjected to the following transformations: translation, central symmetry, axial symmetry and rotation.

Tip: The rotation generally relies on the principle that sum of the angles in a triangle add up to 180 degrees.

- **Ellipse/parabola**

A good knowledge of constructions related to focal points and tangents is required in relation to the ellipse. Inscribing a parabola in a rectangle is always examined.

Tip: Be aware of the construction required to construct an ellipse when just one axis and a point on the curve are given.

- **Solids in mutual contact**

You may be asked to draw cones, spheres and cylinders in mutual contact showing the exact contact points.

The question is sometimes combined with surface development.

Section B – Ordinary level

- **Orthographic projection**

Two views of a given isometric drawing of an object are required in this question. Four main dimensions must be added using a standard dimensioning method.

Tip: Ensure that the end view or plan is correctly positioned relative to the elevation.

- **Ellipse**

Be familiar with a method of drawing an ellipse when the major and minor axes are given. The major axis may be vertical or horizontal.

Tip: Ensure that the freehand curves are of high quality to improve your marks.

- **Surface development**

Two views of an object which contain part of a cylinder are generally required in part (a) of the question. A full one piece surface development is always required in part (b).

Tip: Divide the circular end of the cylinder to determine the length of the curved surface accurately.

- **Transformations**

In this question a simple shape is subjected to the following transformations: translation, central symmetry, axial symmetry.

Tip: Start by drawing the question exactly as it appears on the examination paper.

- **Tangents**

Accuracy is the key feature of this question. It frequently includes an arc, the centre of which may be located by bisecting 2 chords.

Tip: The correct method must always be shown for locating the exact contact points.

- **Oblique or Isometric drawing**

This question will be presented in a grid format with outline dimensions and the correct angles must be used to draw the 3 dimensional view.

Tip: It is generally easier and quicker to draw the oblique view.

On the examination day

Read the each question carefully before you commence the solution and attempt all parts of each question as requested. **Neatness and presentation skills are very important in the examination.** Approximately 14% of the marks for each question in Section B are awarded for this.

- Number each question neatly in section B.

- You may place one or more questions on each A2 sheet. Ensure sufficient space is left for end views or other projections.

- Draw light construction lines initially with a 2H grade pencil.

- You may attempt an extra question if time allows. Examiners will mark all questions and omit your weakest attempt.

- Write your examination number in the space provided on each drawing sheet.

Examination Paper Analysis

Section A – Higher Level

Topic	2019	2018	2017	2016	2015	2014	2013	2012	2011	2010	2009	2008	2007	2006
Geometry	✓	✓	✓		✓	✓	✓		✓	✓	✓	✓	✓	✓
Orthographic	✓	✓	✓	✓		✓	✓	✓	✓	✓	✓	✓	✓	
Perspective	✓	✓	✓	✓	✓	✓	✓	✓	✓	✓	✓	✓	✓	
Sketching	✓	✓	✓	✓	✓	✓	✓	✓	✓	✓	✓	✓	✓	✓
Areas		✓					✓		✓			✓	✓	
Ellipse		✓	✓	✓		✓	✓	✓			✓			
Truncation							✓	✓	✓	✓				
CAD	✓	✓	✓	✓	✓	✓	✓	✓	✓	✓	✓	✓	✓	✓
Angles	✓	✓	✓		✓	✓	✓	✓	✓	✓	✓	✓	✓	
Tangents	✓	✓	✓	✓	✓	✓	✓	✓	✓	✓	✓	✓	✓	✓
Aux. Elev.	✓	✓	✓		✓	✓	✓	✓	✓	✓		✓		
Graphs	✓	✓	✓	✓	✓	✓	✓	✓	✓	✓	✓	✓	✓	✓
Surface Dev.	✓			✓	✓				✓		✓	✓		✓
Rotation	✓	✓	✓	✓	✓	✓			✓	✓	✓	✓	✓	
Symmetry				✓		✓			✓	✓	✓			✓
Division					✓			✓	✓					
Counting blocks										✓		✓	✓	✓
Pictograms														✓
Similar shapes	✓		✓		✓	✓								✓
Axonometric					✓	✓								
Matching drawings	✓	✓		✓	✓									
Parabola	✓				✓									
Shadows		✓	✓		✓									
Solids in contact		✓			✓									
Revolved solids					✓									
Ratio			✓	✓										

Student Study Essentials

Section B – Higher Level

Topic	2007	2008	2009	2010	2011	2012	2013	2014	2015	2016	2017	2018	2019
Orthographic Projection True Shape	Semi-ellipse in plan	Ellipse in plan	Semi-ellipse in plan	Semi-ellipse in elevation	Semi-ellipse in end view	Ellipse in end view	Semi-ellipse in plan	Semi-ellipse in plan	Ellipse in end view	Semi-ellipse in elevation	Semi-ellipse in plan True shape	Semi-ellipse in elevation True shape	Semi-ellipse in plan True shape
Rotated surface	Project End view	Project End view	Project End view	Project elevation	Project Plan	Project End view	Project End view	Project End view	Project Plan	Project End view	Project an elevation	Project an end view	Project Plan
Axonometric projection	Circle included	Circle included	Circle included	Circle included	Circle included	Circle included	Circle included	Circle included	Includes 2 circles	Given elev. & end view	Given elev. plan, circles	Given elev. plan, circle included	Given elev. & end view
Surface Development	Pyramid Cone	Cylinder	–	Cylinder	Cone Cylinder	Cone Cylinder	Pyramid Cylinder	Cone	Cone Cylinder	Cone Cylinder	Truncated Pyramid	Truncated cone and cylinder	Truncated cone and semicircle
Transformations	Translation Central Axial Rotation	Translation Central Axial Rotation	Translation Central Axial Rotation	Translation Central Axial Rotation	Translation Central Axial Rotation	Translation Central Axial Rotation	Translation Central Axial Rotation	Translation Central Axial Rotation	Translation Central Axial Rotation	Translation Central Axial Rotation	Translation Central Axial Rotation	Translation Central Axial Rotation	Translation Central Axial Rotation
Ellipse parabola	Major axis Point on curve	Major axis Point Tangent	Major axis Point on curve	Major axis focus Tangent	Major axis and Point Tangent	Minor axis and focus Tangent	Major axis and point Tangent	Minor axis and focus	Given Focal Pts. point on curve, normal parabola	Minor axis, Point on curve, Tangents Parabola	Minor axis and focus. Normals to ellipse Parabola	Major axis and point on curve. Tangent to ellipse Parabola	Given Major axis and focus. Tangent from external point Parabola
Solids in contact		Cylinder hemi-sphere	Cone Sphere Pyramid	–	–	–	–	Cone Sphere	–		Pyramid Sphere, cylinder		Truncated cone and sphere

Section A – Ordinary Level

Topic	2019	2018	2017	2016	2015	2014	2013	2012	2011	2010	2009	2008	2007	2006
Geometry			✓		✓					✓				
Orthographic	✓	✓	✓	✓	✓	✓	✓	✓	✓	✓	✓	✓	✓	✓
Perspective	✓	✓	✓		✓	✓	✓	✓	✓	✓	✓	✓	✓	✓
Sketching	✓	✓	✓	✓	✓	✓	✓	✓	✓	✓	✓	✓	✓	✓
Areas	✓	✓	✓	✓	✓	✓	✓	✓	✓	✓	✓	✓	✓	✓
Ellipse	✓	✓	✓	✓	✓	✓	✓	✓	✓	✓	✓	✓	✓	✓
CAD	✓	✓	✓	✓	✓	✓	✓	✓	✓	✓	✓	✓	✓	✓
Computers	✓	✓		✓			✓	✓	✓	✓	✓	✓		✓
Tangents	✓	✓	✓	✓	✓	✓	✓	✓	✓			✓	✓	✓
Isometric	✓	✓			✓	✓		✓	✓			✓		✓
Shadows		✓					✓	✓	✓	✓	✓	✓	✓	✓
Polygons		✓	✓			✓	✓	✓		✓		✓		✓
Rotation								✓	✓	✓	✓	✓	✓	
Symmetry			✓	✓	✓	✓	✓							
Aux. Elev.												✓	✓	✓
Scales	✓	✓	✓	✓	✓	✓	✓	✓	✓	✓	✓	✓	✓	✓
Enlarging	✓	✓	✓	✓	✓	✓	✓	✓	✓					
Digital			✓			✓								
Electrical device				✓	✓									
Graphs	✓		✓	✓	✓									
Line Division	✓													
Counting Blocks	✓													

Section B – Ordinary Level

Topic	2019	2018	2017	2016	2015	2014	2013	2012	2011	2010	2009	2008	2007
Orthographic Dimensioning	✓	✓	✓	✓	✓	✓	✓	✓	✓	✓	✓	✓	✓
Ellipse	✓	✓	✓	✓	✓	✓	✓	✓	✓	✓	✓	✓	✓
Surface Development	✓	✓	✓	✓	✓	✓	✓	✓	✓	✓	✓	✓	✓
Transformations	Translation, Central Axial	Translation, Central Axial	Translation, Central Axial	Translation Central Axial	Translation Central Axial	Translation Central Axial	Translation Central Axial	Translation Central Axial	Translation Central Axial	Translation Central Axial	Translation Central Axial	Translation Central Axial	Translation Central Axial
Oblique/ Isometric	✓	✓	✓	✓	✓	✓	✓	✓	✓	✓	✓	✓	✓
Tangents	✓	✓	✓	✓	✓	✓	✓	✓	✓		✓	✓	✓

Map Your Progress!

Tick each question as you complete it and also tick when you have completed the entire exam paper.

JUNIOR CERTIFICATE TECHNICAL GRAPHICS	TIME	2019	2018	2017	2016	2015	2014	2013	2012	2011	2010
HIGHER LEVEL	3 hours										
Section A (120 marks) Answer 10 questions	4 minutes per question										
Section B (280 marks) Answer 4 questions	35 minutes per question										
Question 1											
Question 2											
Question 3											
Question 4											
Question 5											
Question 6											
Exam Complete											

(Continued)

JUNIOR CERTIFICATE TECHNICAL GRAPHICS	TIME	2019	2018	2017	2016	2015	2014	2013	2012	2011	2010
ORDINARY LEVEL	2.5 hours										
Section A (120 marks) Answer 10 questions	3 minutes per question										
Section B (280 marks) Answer 4 question	30 minutes per question										
Question 1											
Question 2											
Question 3											
Question 4											
Question 5											
Question 6											
Exam Complete											

Junior Cert Grades Chart

Percentage Range	Grade
85 or over	A
70 but less than 85	B
55 but less than 70	C
40 but less than 55	D
25 but less than 40	E
10 but less than 25	F
Less than 10	No Grade

Source: State Examinations Commission, 2019.

STUDY HUB

Your free online guide to smarter study.
Visit
www.edco.ie/onlinestudyhub

Remember:

↻ Answer section A directly on this book (12 Marks for each question)
↻ Answer Section B on A2 paper (70 marks for each question)
↻ Presentation is very important in both sections

Student Study Essentials © The Educational Company of Ireland, 2019

Coimisiún na Scrúduithe Stáit
State Examinations Commission

Junior Certificate Examination, 2019

Technical Graphics
Higher Level
Section A
(120 marks)

Monday, 17 June
Morning, 9:30 - 12:30

Centre Number

Instructions

(a)   Answer **any ten** questions in the spaces provided. All questions carry equal marks.

(b)   Construction lines must be clearly shown.

(c)   All measurements are in millimetres.

(d)   This booklet must be handed up at the end of the examination.

(e)   Write your examination number in the box provided below and on all other pages used.

Question	Mark
Section A	
1	
2	
3	
4	
5	
6	
TOTAL	
GRADE	

Examination Number:

SECTION A. Answer **any ten** questions. All questions carry equal marks.

1. Fill in the label for **each** diagram by selecting from the given list.

- Chord
- Sector
- Quadrant
- Tangent

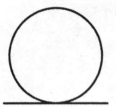 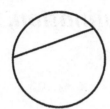 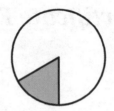 

1. _____ 2. _____ 3. _____ 4. _____

2. The figure shows the incomplete perspective drawing of an electric piano. A 3D graphic is also shown. Complete the perspective drawing.

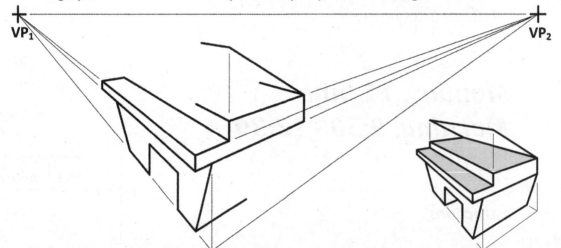

3. The figure shows the outline of a pair of 3D cinema glasses based on two regular pentagons.

Write down the measurements of **A**, **B** and **C**.

A = _____

B = _____

C = _____

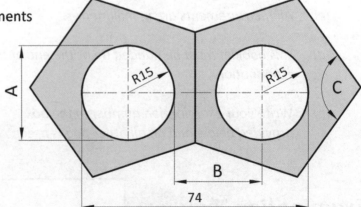

4. The elevation and end view of a weighing scales are shown on the square grid.
Make a **freehand pictorial sketch** of the weighing scales. Colour **or** shade the sketch.

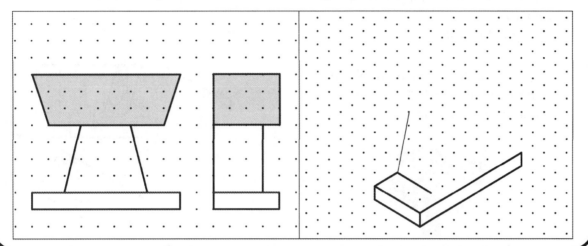

5. Shown is a graphical puzzle consisting of **squares**, **rectangles** and **triangles**.
Count the number of **squares**, **rectangles** and **triangles**.

Squares   _____

Rectangles   _____

Triangles   _____

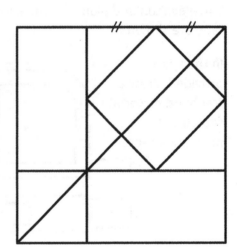

6. The figure below shows the elevation of a stapler. A 3D graphic is also shown.

Rotate **ABCDE** about point **O** until point **E** reaches the line **LL₁**.

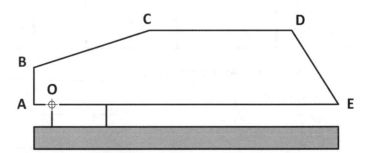

3

7. The figure shows the outline elevation and plan of a security camera.
A 3D graphic is also shown.

Project an auxiliary elevation of the camera on the line X_1-Y_1 to show the true shape of surface **S**.

8. The elevation and plan of a measuring tape are shown.

In the space provided, draw a **freehand pictorial sketch** of the measuring tape.

Colour **or** shade the completed sketch.

9. Write down **any three** CAD commands used to edit the drawing of the picture frame as shown in the sequence below.

Any **three** CAD commands: _____

_____

_____

4

10. **Fig. 1** shows a design for a glamping pod. Shown in **Fig. 2** is the incomplete elevation of the glamping pod.

Complete the elevation in **Fig. 2** by constructing a parabola in the rectangle **ABCD** with its vertex at **O**.

Show clearly all construction.

Fig. 1

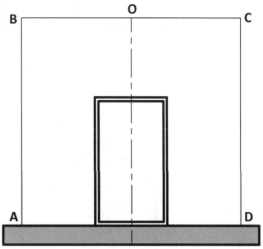

Fig. 2

---

11. **Fig. 1** shows the development of an object.

Three images of objects **before** development are shown on the right.

From the images on the right match the letter for the development shown in **Fig. 1**.

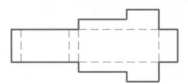

Fig. 1 = _____

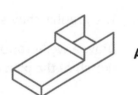

A

B

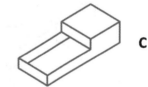

C

---

12. The incomplete outline of a shelf support is shown. A 3D graphic of the support is also shown.

Complete the outline of the support by constructing the internal tangent to the two given circles.

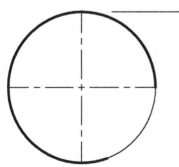

5

13. The figure shows the outline of a house.
Draw a new outline similar to the given house, with the length **AB** increased to **AB₁**.

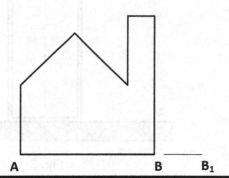

A   B   B₁

14. The graphic shows a set of steps.

Draw a well-proportioned **freehand** sketch of the **plan** of the steps.

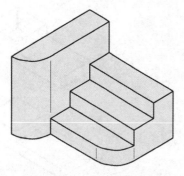

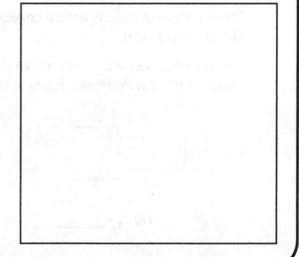

15. Car sales in a garage were recorded over a period of six months.
The following are the results:

- January - 50
- February - 30
- March - 55
- April - 15
- May - 25
- June - 45

Complete the chart to represent this information graphically.

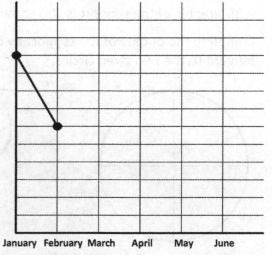

January February March April May June

6

Coimisiún na Scrúduithe Stáit
State Examinations Commission

Junior Certificate Examination, 2019

Technical Graphics
Higher Level
Section B

(280 marks)

Monday, 17 June
Morning, 9:30 - 12:30

Instructions

(a)   Answer **any four** questions.

(b)   Construction lines must be clearly shown.

(c)   All questions in this section carry equal marks.

(d)   The number of the question must be distinctly written by the side of each answer.

(e)   Work on **one side** of the paper only.

(f)   Write your examination number on each sheet of paper used.

SECTION B. Answer **any four** questions. All questions carry equal marks.

1. A pictorial view of a mobile lunar camera is shown in **Fig. 1**.
Also shown is a 3D graphic of the camera.

(a) Draw an elevation in the direction of arrow **A**.

(b) Project a plan from the elevation.

(c) Project an end view in the direction of arrow **B**.

(d) Determine the true shape of surface **S**.

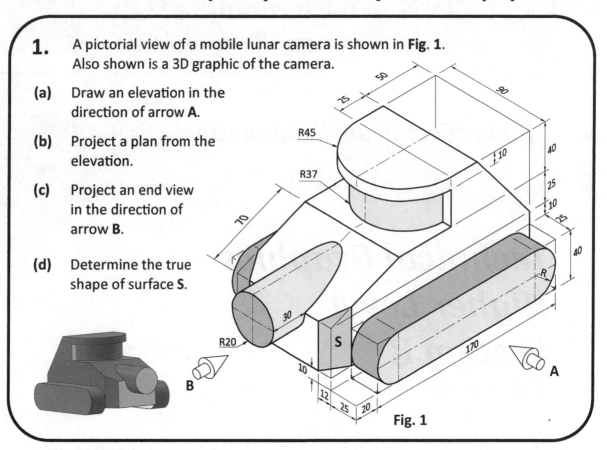

Fig. 1

2. The elevation, end view and a 3D graphic of a sign for a coffee shop are shown.
The sign includes a semi-octagon **ABCDEF**. The line **EG** is a tangent from **E**.
The curve **JKL** is a circular arc. The curve **QRS** is concentric with **JKL**.

(a) Draw the given elevation and end view.

The sign is rotated through 45° about point **O**, as shown by the broken line in end view.

(b) Project a plan to show the sign in the rotated position.

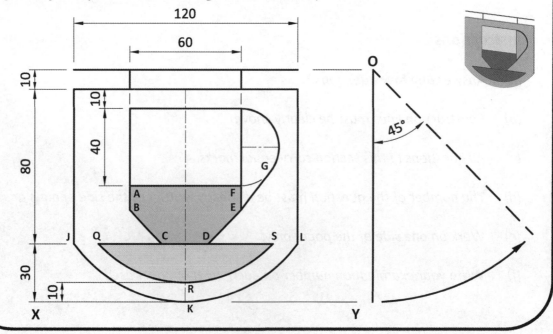

8

3. The axonometric axes required for the isometric projection of a petrol pump are shown. The elevation, end view and a 3D graphic of the pump are also shown.

(a)

(i) Draw the axonometric axes as shown.

(ii) Draw the given elevation inclined at 15° as shown.

(iii) Draw the given end view inclined at 15° as shown.

(iv) Draw the completed axonometric projection of the petrol pump.

OR

(b) Draw the isometric projection of the petrol pump using the isometric scale method.

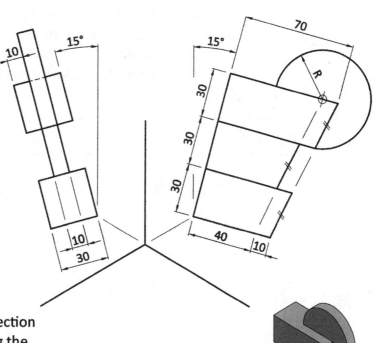

4. The elevation and plan of a sand bucket and beach ball are shown. A 3D graphic of the bucket and ball is also shown. The bucket and ball consist of a truncated inverted cone **A** and a sphere **B** respectively.

The sphere rests on the horizontal plane and is in contact with the truncated cone. The bucket has a semi-circular handle **S** positioned as shown in plan and elevation.

(a) Draw the given elevation and plan, showing all constructions and points of contact.

(b) Draw the development of the conical surface **A**.

(c) Draw the development of the semi-circular handle **S**.

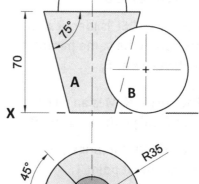

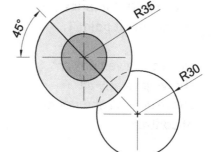

9

5. The figure shows the logo for a lighting company.
The logo is subject to transformations in the following order:

- Axial Symmetry **P - P₁**
- Central Symmetry **P₁ - P₂**
- Translation **P₂ - P₃**
- Rotation anti-clockwise through 90° from **P₃ - P₄**

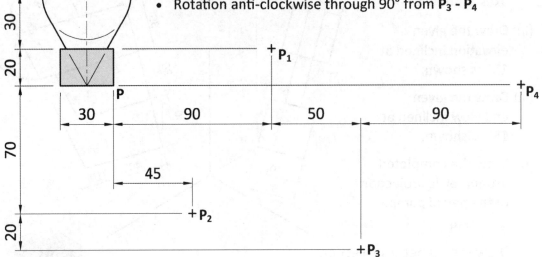

(a) Draw the given figure.

(b) Determine and draw the image of the logo under **each** of the above transformations.

Note: *All geometric constructions must be clearly shown on your drawing sheet.*

---

6. The figure shows a design for a rugby trophy.

The curve **ABC** is a parabola with vertex at **B**.

The curve **DEF** is identical to a portion of the same parabola with vertex at **E**.

The curve **JKLM** is an ellipse with focal points at **N** and **P**.

The line **BT** is a tangent to the ellipse at point **T**.

Draw the given design showing clearly all constructions and points of contact.

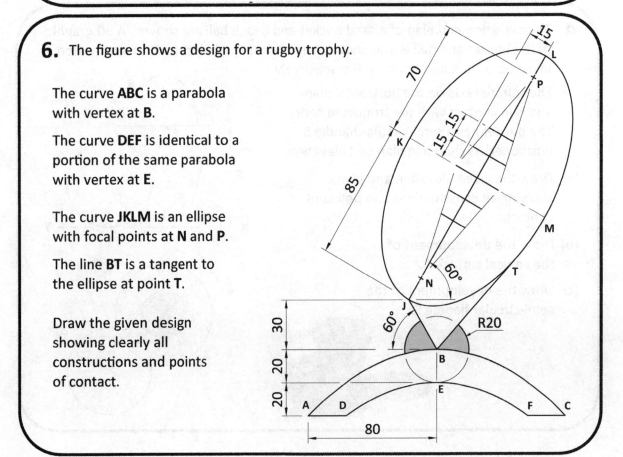

2018 HL

Coimisiún na Scrúduithe Stáit
State Examinations Commission

Junior Certificate Examination, 2018

Technical Graphics
Higher Level
Section A

(120 marks)

Monday, 18 June
Morning, 9:30 - 12:30

Centre Number

Instructions

(a)   Answer **any ten** questions in the spaces provided.
All questions carry equal marks.

(b)   Construction lines must be clearly shown.

(c)   All measurements are in millimetres.

(d)   This booklet must be handed up at the end of the
examination.

(e)   Write your examination number in the box
provided below and on all other pages used.

Examination Number:

Question	Mark
Section A	
1	
2	
3	
4	
5	
6	
TOTAL	
GRADE	

SECTION A. Answer **any ten** questions. All questions carry equal marks.

---

1. Fill in the label for **each** diagram by selecting from the given list.

- Trapezoid
- Octagon
- Hexagon
- Parallelogram

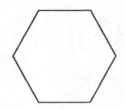 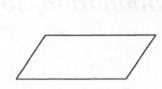 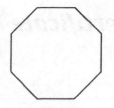 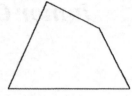

1. _____ 2. _____ 3. _____ 4. _____

---

2. The figure shows the incomplete perspective drawing of a gymnastics pommel horse. A 3D graphic is also shown. Complete the perspective drawing.

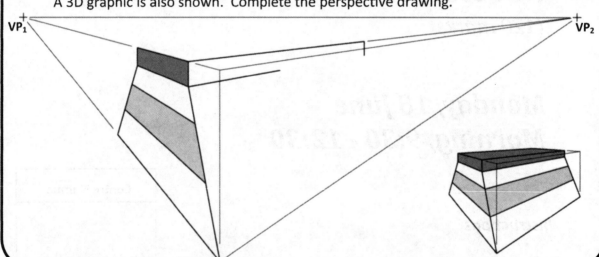

---

3. The figure shows the outline of a mathematical symbol.

Write down the measurements of the angles marked **A**, **B** and **C**.

A = _____

B = _____

C = _____

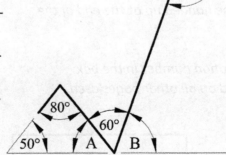

12

4. The elevation and end view of a barbeque are shown on the square grid.
Make a **freehand pictorial sketch** of the barbeque. Colour **or** shade the sketch.

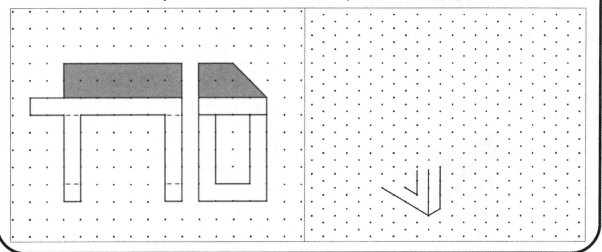

5. The surface area of road markings, similar to that shown in the 3D graphic, is specified by law. The figure shows the triangular outline **ABC** of a directional road marking. Convert the triangle **ABC** to a rectangle of equal area.

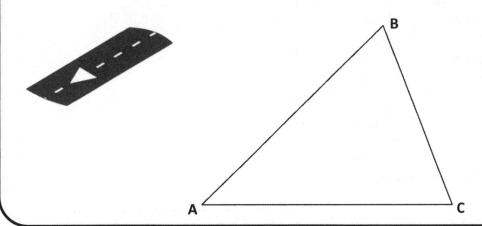

6. The figure shows an elevation of a gavel and block as used by a judge in court.
Also shown is a 3D graphic of the gavel and block.

Rotate the gavel **abcd** about point **O** until it reaches the top surface **LL₁** of the block.

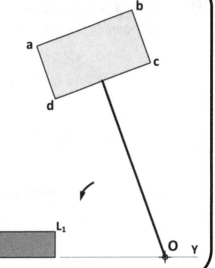

7. The figure shows the elevation and plan of a lectern.

A 3D graphic of the lectern is also shown.

Project an auxiliary elevation of the lectern on the line X_1-Y_1 to show the true shape of surface **S**.

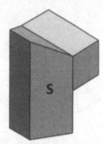

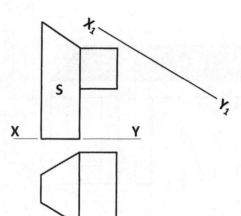

8. The elevation and plan of a date stamp are shown.

In the space provided, draw a **freehand pictorial sketch** of the stamp.

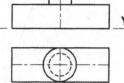

Colour **or** shade the completed sketch.

9. Write down **any three** CAD commands used to edit the drawing of the hall mirror, as shown in the sequence below.

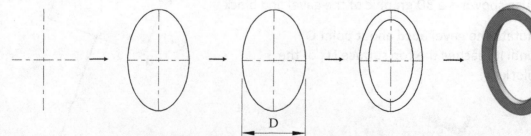

Any **three** CAD commands: _____

_____

_____

10. Shown is the outline elevation and incomplete plan of an *angry bird* character in contact with a sloping block.

A 3D graphic is also shown.

Draw the plan of the sphere and locate the point of contact between the sphere and block.

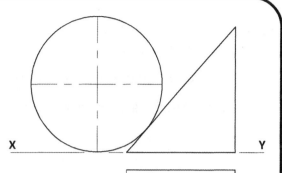

11. **Fig.1** shows a logo for a telephone company. The curve **abc** is based on a semi-ellipse. **Fig. 2** shows the location of the axes and focal points of the semi-ellipse. The point **P** is a point on the curve.

Determine the lengths of the major and minor axes and complete the drawing of the logo.

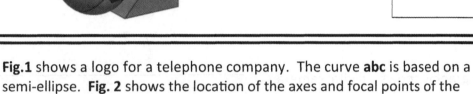

Fig.1

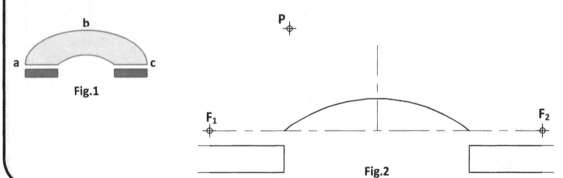

Fig.2

12. The graphic below shows three stacking puzzles. The plan of each puzzle is shown on the right.

Match the correct letter with the appropriate puzzle below.

A

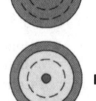

B

C

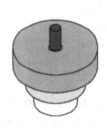

1. _____   2. _____   3. _____

13. The graphics show the design of a door mirror for a car.

The centres of the arcs are shown.

Show clearly **all** points of contact.

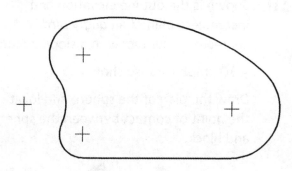

14. The graphic shows a digital camera.

Draw a well-proportioned **freehand** sketch of the **elevation** of the camera viewed in the direction of the arrow.

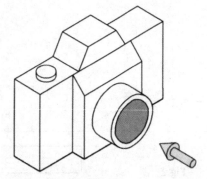

15. Twenty four tourists were surveyed while visiting a village in Ireland.

The following were the nationalities of the tourists surveyed:

United Kingdom	-	12
United States	-	6
Germany	-	3
France	-	3

Divide the given circle to represent this information graphically as a pie chart.

Colour **or** shade the completed pie chart.

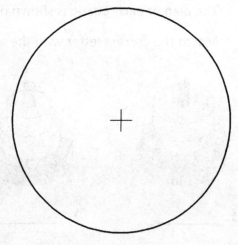

Coimisiún na Scrúduithe Stáit
State Examinations Commission

Junior Certificate Examination, 2018

Technical Graphics
Higher Level
Section B
(280 marks)

Monday, 18 June
Morning, 9:30 - 12:30

Instructions

(a)   Answer **any four** questions.

(b)   Construction lines must be clearly shown.

(c)   All questions in this section carry equal marks.

(d)   The number of the question must be distinctly marked by the side of each answer.

(e)   Work on **one side** of the paper only.

(f)   Write your examination number on each sheet of paper used.

SECTION B. Answer **any four** questions. All questions carry equal marks.

1. A pictorial view of an airport terminal is shown.
Also shown is a 3D graphic of the terminal.

(a) Draw an elevation in the direction of arrow **A**.

(b) Project a plan from the elevation.

(c) Project an end view in the direction of arrow **B**.

(d) Determine the true shape of surface **S**.

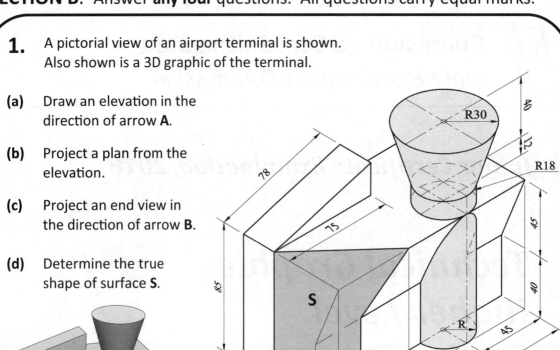

2. The elevation, plan and 3D graphic of a logo for a hot air balloon club are shown.

The logo is based on a regular pentagon **ABCDE** and tangents **QP** and **QR** to the circle at points **P** and **R** respectively.

(a) Draw the given elevation and plan.

The logo is rotated through 40° about point **O** as shown by the broken line in plan.

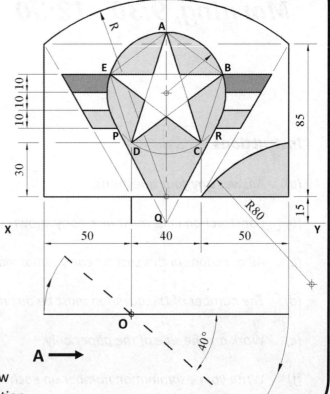

(b) Project an end view in the direction of arrow **A** to show the logo in the rotated position.

18

3. The axonometric axes required for the isometric projection of a cash register are shown. The elevation, plan and a 3D graphic of the register are also shown.

(a)

(i) Draw the axonometric axes as shown.

(ii) Draw the given elevation inclined at 15° as shown.

(iii) Draw the given plan inclined at 45° as shown.

(iv) Draw the completed axonometric projection of the cash register.

OR

(b) Draw the isometric projection of the cash register using the isometric scale method.

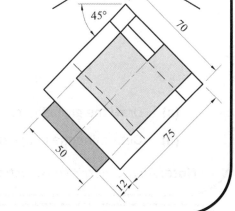

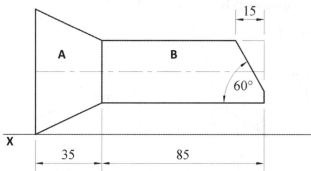

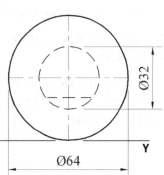

4. The elevation and end view of a torch are shown. The torch consists of a truncated cone **A** and a cylinder **B**, which is also truncated as shown.

A 3D graphic of the torch is also shown.

(a) Draw the given elevation and end view.

(b) Project a plan from the elevation.

(c) Draw a development of the conical surface **A**.

(d) Draw a development of the cylindrical surface **B**.

19

5. The figure shows a logo for a locksmith shop.

The logo is subject to transformations in the following order:

- Axial Symmetry **P - P₁**
- Translation **P₁ - P₂**
- Central Symmetry **P₂ - P₃**
- Rotation clockwise about point **O** until point **P₃** reaches the line **OL**.

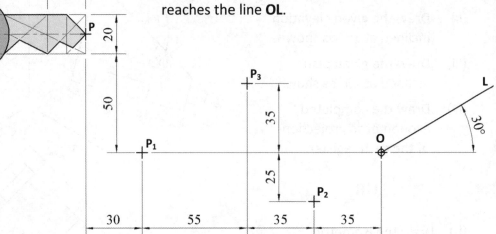

(a) Draw the given figure.

(b) Determine the image of the logo under **each** of the above transformations.

Note: *All geometric constructions must be clearly shown on your drawing sheet.*

---

6. The figure shows a design for a toy loading-shovel.

The curve **ABCD** is portion of an ellipse with major axis **AD**. Point **B** is a point on the curve. Determine the length of the minor axis and draw the ellipse.

The curve **UV**, with vertex at **U** is an identical portion of the same ellipse.

The line **BT** is a tangent to the ellipse at **B**.

The curve **KMN** is a parabola with vertex at **M**.

Draw the given design showing clearly all constructions and points of contact.

Coimisiún na Scrúduithe Stáit
State Examinations Commission

Junior Certificate Examination, 2017

Technical Graphics
Higher Level
Section A
(120 marks)

Monday, 19 June
Morning, 9:30 - 12:30

Centre Number

Instructions

(a)   Answer **any ten** questions in the spaces provided. All questions carry equal marks.

(b)   Construction lines must be clearly shown.

(c)   All measurements are in millimetres.

(d)   This booklet must be handed up at the end of the examination.

(e)   Write your examination number in the box provided below and on all other pages used.

Question	Mark
Section A	
1	
2	
3	
4	
5	
6	
TOTAL	
GRADE	

Examination Number:

SECTION A. Answer **any ten** questions. All questions carry equal marks.

1. Fill in the label for **each** diagram by selecting from the given list.

- Eccentric
- Sector
- Segment
- Concentric

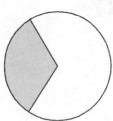 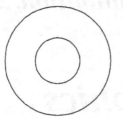 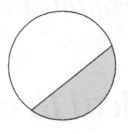 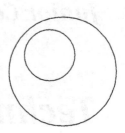

1. _____   2. _____   3. _____   4. _____

2. The figure shows the incomplete perspective drawing of an ice-hockey table. A 3D graphic is also shown. Complete the perspective drawing.

VP₁

VP₂

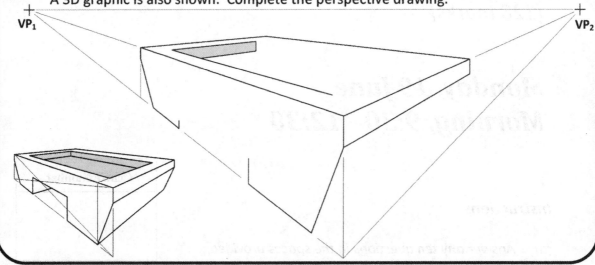

3. The figure shows the outline of a logo for a locksmith.

Write down the measurements of **A**, **B** and **C**.

A = _____

B = _____

C = _____

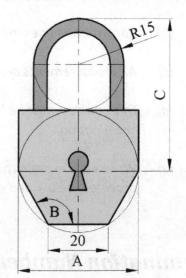

4. The elevation and end view of a keyboard are shown on the square grid.
Make a **freehand pictorial sketch** of the keyboard. Colour **or** shade the sketch.

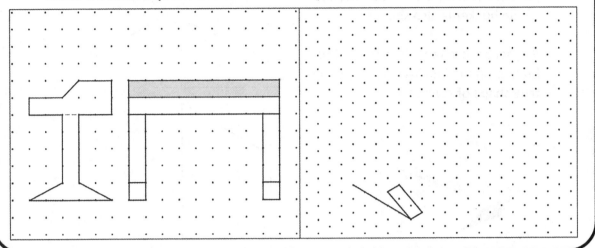

5. The figure shows the design of a lampshade.
Draw a new shade similar to the given shade, with the length **AB** increased to **AB₁**.

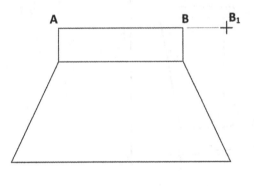

6. **Fig 1.** shows a 3D graphic of a set of triangular flags.
Each flag is an equilateral triangle. The length of side of each flag reduces in the ratio **3:2:1**.

Fig 2. shows the incomplete elevation of the flags.

Find the length of side of each flag and complete the elevation.

Fig. 1

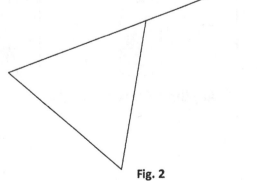

Fig. 2

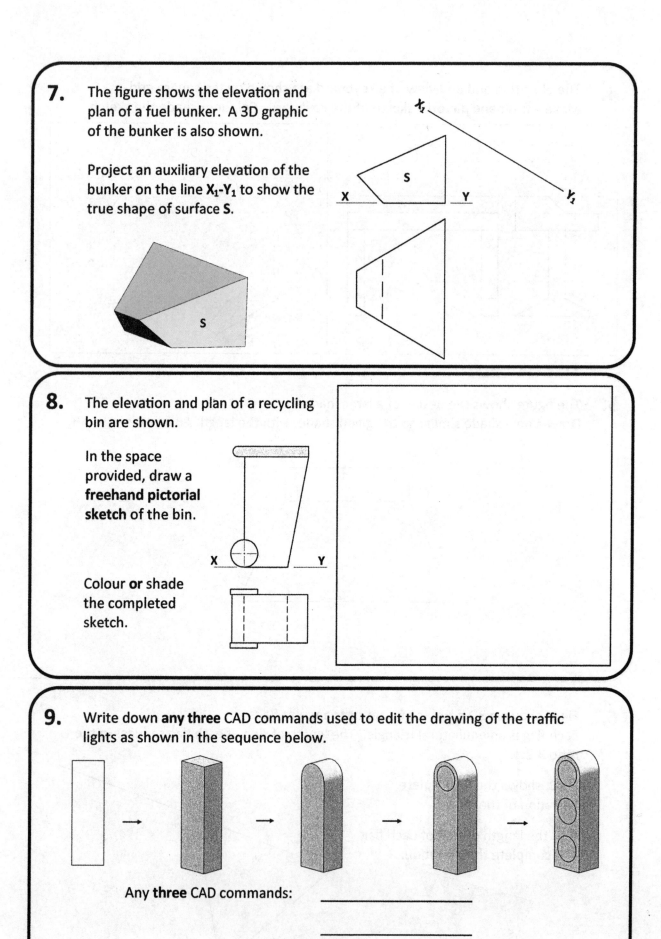

7. The figure shows the elevation and plan of a fuel bunker. A 3D graphic of the bunker is also shown.

Project an auxiliary elevation of the bunker on the line X_1-Y_1 to show the true shape of surface **S**.

8. The elevation and plan of a recycling bin are shown.

In the space provided, draw a **freehand pictorial sketch** of the bin.

Colour **or** shade the completed sketch.

9. Write down **any three** CAD commands used to edit the drawing of the traffic lights as shown in the sequence below.

Any **three** CAD commands: _____

_____

_____

24

10. The graphics show the design of a cyclist's time-trial helmet.
The design includes an ellipse **A** and a tangent **BC**.

Locate the focal points of the ellipse **A** and determine the point of contact between the tangent **BC** and the ellipse.

Show clearly all constructions.

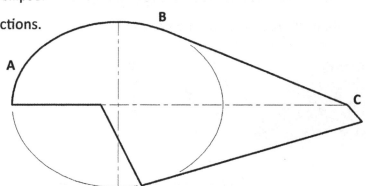

---

11. The figure below shows the elevation of an adjustable set-square.
A 3D graphic is also shown.

Rotate **ABCD** about point **O** until point **C** reaches the line **LL₁**.

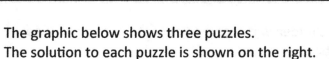

---

12. The graphic below shows three puzzles.
The solution to each puzzle is shown on the right.

Match the correct letter with the appropriate puzzle below.

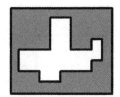

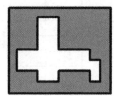

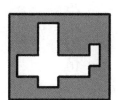

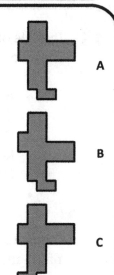

1. _____   2. _____   3. _____

25

13. The 3D graphic shows a football as it strikes the back of a goal net. Also shown is an end view of the goal net and a football **O**.

Draw the football in position when it strikes the back of the net and rests on the ground **GG₁**.

Show all constructions and points of contact.

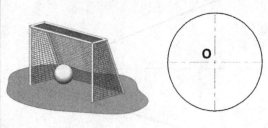 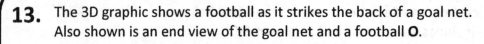 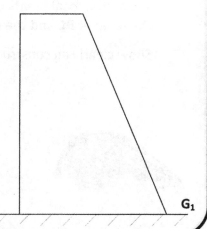

G   G₁

14. The graphic shows three **solids**. Light is shining on the solids, as shown by the direction of the arrow. The shadow cast by the first solid has been completed.

Draw **freehand sketches** of the shadows cast by the other two solids.

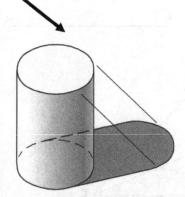  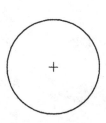

15. The sale of fruit in a school canteen was recorded over the period of a week. The following are the results:

- Apple - 60
- Banana - 45
- Grape - 25
- Kiwi - 20
- Orange - 40
- Pear - 10

Complete the chart to represent this information graphically.

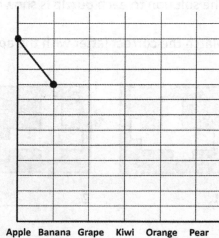

Apple Banana Grape Kiwi Orange Pear

Coimisiún na Scrúduithe Stáit
State Examinations Commission

Junior Certificate Examination, 2017

Technical Graphics
Higher Level
Section B
(280 marks)

Monday, 19 June
Morning, 9:30 - 12:30

Instructions

(a)   Answer **any four** questions.

(b)   Construction lines must be clearly shown.

(c)   All questions in this section carry equal marks.

(d)   The number of the question must be distinctly marked by the side of each answer.

(e)   Work on **one side** of the paper only.

(f)   Write your examination number on each sheet of paper used.

SECTION B. Answer **any four** questions. All questions carry equal marks.

1. A pictorial view of a road roller is shown. Also shown is a 3D graphic of the roller.

(a) Draw an elevation in the direction of arrow **A**.

(b) Project a plan from the elevation.

(c) Project an end view in the direction of arrow **B**.

(d) Determine the true shape of surface **S**.

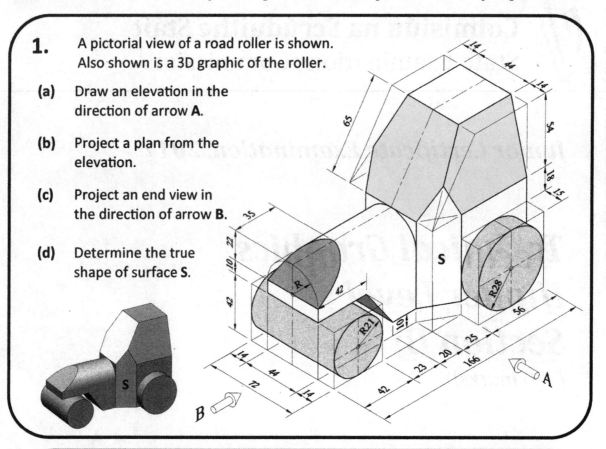

2. The elevation, plan, end view and a 3D graphic of a jewellery box are shown. The logo on lid **A** is based on an equilateral triangle. The mirror on lid **B** is based on a regular octagon.

(a) Draw the given elevation, plan and end view.

The lids are opened separately, lid **A** through 30° and lid **B** through 55° about point **O**, as shown by the two broken lines in end view.

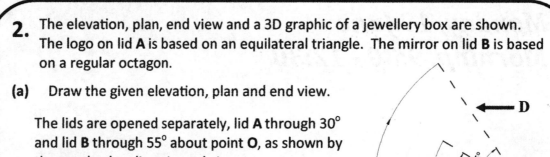

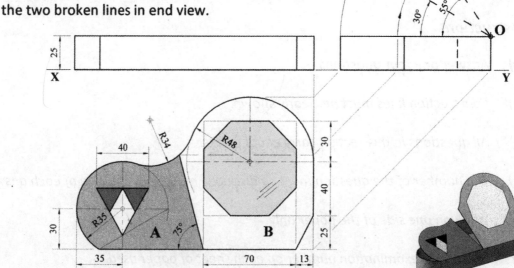

(b) Project an elevation of the lids in the direction of arrow **D** to show **both** lids in their rotated positions.

28

3. The axonometric axes required for the isometric projection of an exercise treadmill are shown. The elevation, plan and a 3D graphic of the treadmill are also shown.

(a)

(i) Draw the axonometric axes as shown.

(ii) Draw the given elevation inclined at 15° as shown.

(iii) Draw the given plan inclined at 45° as shown.

(iv) Draw the completed axonometric projection of the treadmill.

OR

(b) Draw the isometric projection of the treadmill using the isometric scale method.

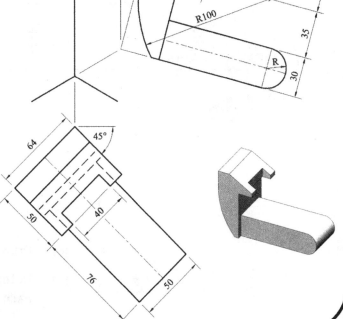

4. The elevation and plan of three beauty products in mutual contact are shown. A 3D graphic of the cylindrical lipstick, spherical cream container and perfume bottle in the form of a square-based pyramid is also shown.

(a) Draw the given elevation and plan, showing all constructions.

(b) Show all points of contact.

(c) Draw the development of the **four** sloping surfaces of the truncated square-based pyramid **A.**

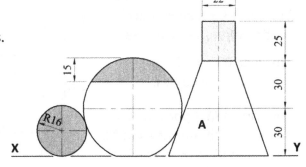

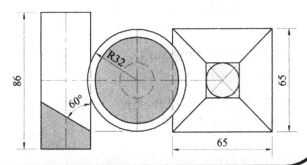

5. The figure shows the logo for a garage.
The logo is subject to transformations in the following order:

- Central Symmetry   **P - P$_1$**
- Axial Symmetry   **P$_1$ - P$_2$**
- Translation   **P$_2$ - P$_3$**
- Rotation about point **O** until point **P$_3$** reaches the line **OL**.

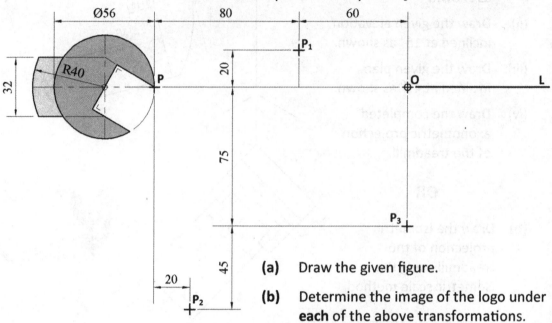

(a) Draw the given figure.

(b) Determine the image of the logo under **each** of the above transformations.

Note: *All geometric constructions must be clearly shown on your drawing sheet.*

---

6. The figure shows a design for a megaphone.

The curve **ABC** is portion of an ellipse with a focal point at **F$_1$**. The curve **EG** is an identical portion of the same ellipse.

The lines **BD** and **GH** are normals to the curves.

The curve **KM** is portion of a parabola with the vertex at **M**. The curve **UV** is portion of an identical parabola with vertex at **V**.

The line **RT** is a tangent to the circle at **T**.

Locate the centre of the arc **KQR** and draw the arc.

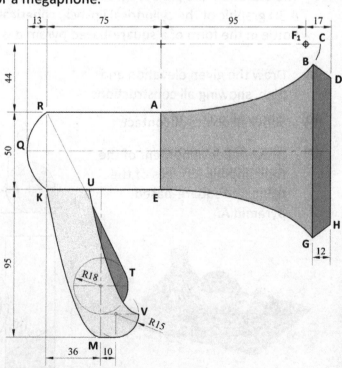

Draw the given design showing clearly all constructions and points of contact.

30

Coimisiún na Scrúduithe Stáit
State Examinations Commission

2016 HL

Junior Certificate Examination, 2016

Technical Graphics
Higher Level
Section A
(120 marks)

Monday, 20 June
Morning, 9:30 - 12:30

Centre Number

Instructions

(a) Answer **any ten** questions in the spaces provided. All questions carry equal marks.

(b) Construction lines must be clearly shown.

(c) All measurements are in millimetres.

(d) This booklet must be handed up at the end of the examination.

(e) Write your examination number in the box provided below and on all other pages used.

Question	Mark
Section A	
1	
2	
3	
4	
5	
6	
TOTAL	
GRADE	

Examination Number:

SECTION A. Answer **any ten** questions. All questions carry equal marks.

1. Fill in the label for **each** developed solid by selecting from the list on the right.

- Cone
- Cylinder
- Triangular prism
- Square-based prism

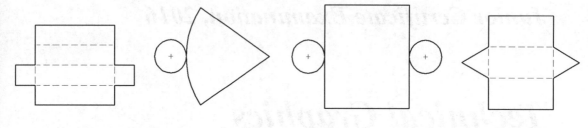

1. _____   2. _____   3. _____   4. _____

2. The figure shows the incomplete perspective drawing of a bird cage. A 3D graphic is also shown. Complete the perspective drawing.

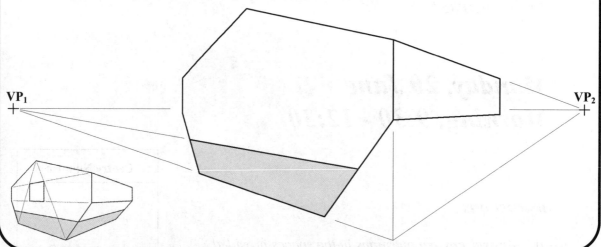

VP₁

VP₂

3. The figure shows the outline of a mini-digger.

Write down the measurements of **A**, **B** and **C**.

A = _____

B = _____

C = _____

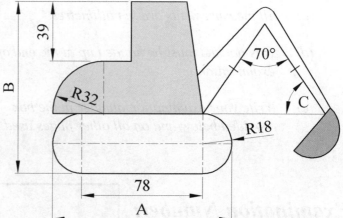

32

4. The elevation and end view of a stool are shown on the square grid.
Make a **freehand pictorial sketch** of the stool. Colour **or** shade the sketch.

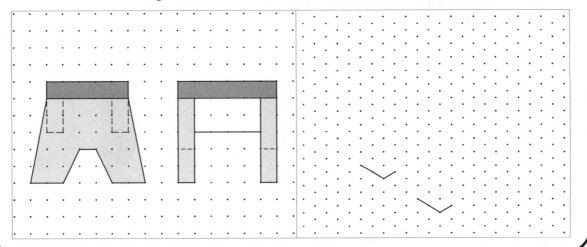

5. The figure below shows the elevation of a skateboard.
A graphic of a skateboard is also shown.

Rotate the skateboard about point **O** until point **A** reaches the line **LL₁**.

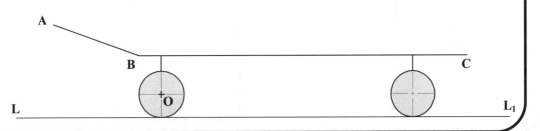

6. The incomplete elevation of a bookcase is shown. Also shown is a 3D graphic of the complete bookcase.

Complete the elevation by:
- dividing the height of the bookcase in the ratio of **3:2:1:1** to find the locations of the shelves
- drawing the shelves in these locations.

7. **Fig. 1** shows a cylinder which has been created by revolving a rectangle about an axis. Complete a freehand sketch of the 3-dimensional solid created when the right-angled triangle in **Fig. 2** and the semi-circle in **Fig. 3** are revolved about their given axis. Name each solid.

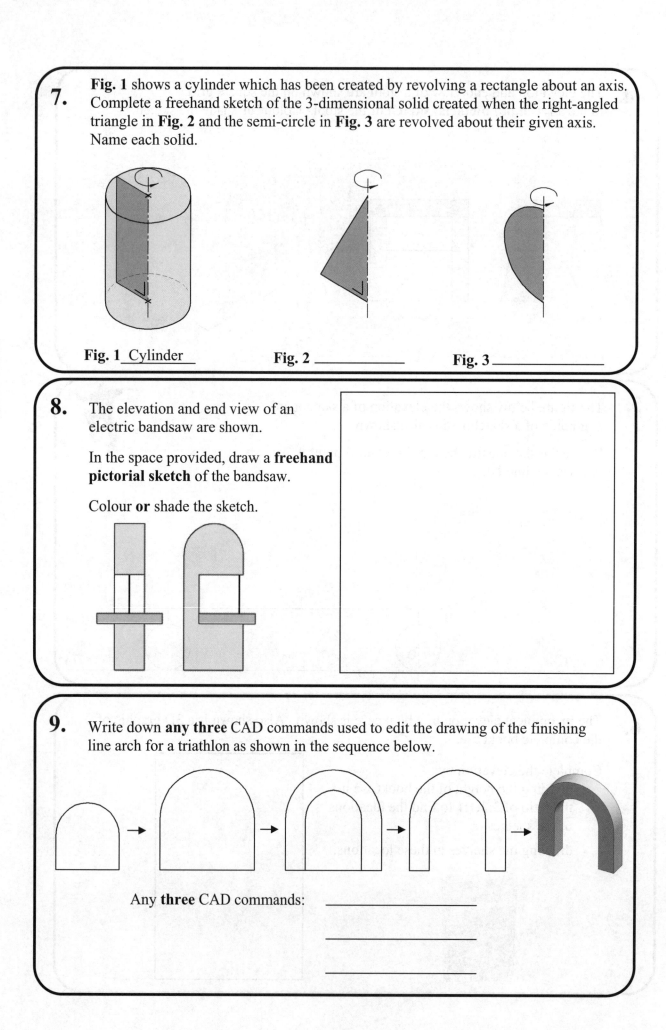

Fig. 1 _Cylinder_   **Fig. 2** _____   **Fig. 3** _____

8. The elevation and end view of an electric bandsaw are shown.

In the space provided, draw a **freehand pictorial sketch** of the bandsaw.

Colour **or** shade the sketch.

9. Write down **any three** CAD commands used to edit the drawing of the finishing line arch for a triathlon as shown in the sequence below.

Any **three** CAD commands: _____

_____

_____

34

10. The 3D graphic shows a water jug. The handle of the jug is a semi-ellipse. The figure shows the location of the axes and focal points of the semi-ellipse.

P is a point on the curve.

Determine the lengths of the major and the minor axes and draw the semi-ellipse.

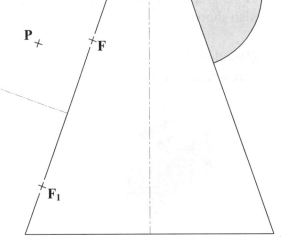

11. The figure shows the elevation and incomplete plan of a set of salt and pepper shakers.

A 3D graphic is also shown.

Complete the given plan and locate the point of contact between the shakers.

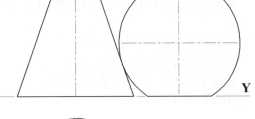

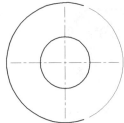

12. The graphic below shows three place settings at a table. The plan of each place setting is shown on the right.

Match the correct letter with the appropriate graphic below.

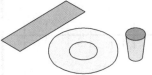

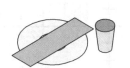

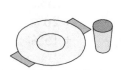

1. _____   2. _____   3. _____

13. The figure shows the elevation, plan and incomplete end view of a toaster.

A 3D graphic of the toaster is also shown.

Complete the end view by constructing the hidden detail.

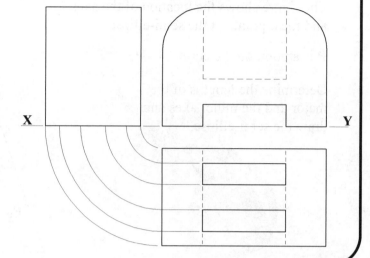

X   Y

14. The incomplete outline of a sports mouthguard is shown. A 3D graphic of the mouthguard is also shown.

Complete the outline of the mouthguard by constructing tangents from points **P** and **Q** to the circle **C**.

Note: *All geometric constructions must be clearly shown.*

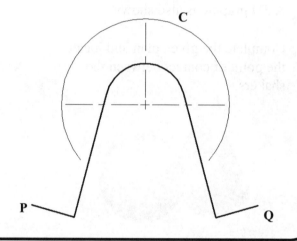

C

P   Q

15. The performance of a student in their Christmas examinations was compared to their performance in the summer examinations. The following changes were recorded:

1. Maths   -   + 10%
2. English   -   - 5%
3. Irish   -   + 30%
4. Science   -   - 15%
5. History   -   + 20%
6. Geography - + 15%

Complete the given chart to represent this information graphically.

Colour **or** shade the completed chart.

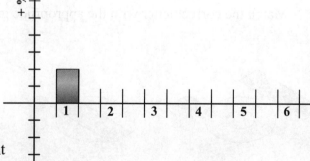

Coimisiún na Scrúduithe Stáit
State Examinations Commission

2016 HL

Junior Certificate Examination, 2016

Technical Graphics
Higher Level
Section B
(280 marks)

Monday, 20 June
Morning, 9:30 - 12:30

Instructions

(a) **Any four** questions to be answered.

(b) All questions in this section carry equal marks.

(c) The number of the question must be distinctly marked by the side of each answer.

(d) Work on **one side** of the paper only.

(e) Write your examination number on each sheet of paper used.

SECTION B. Answer **any four** questions. All questions carry equal marks.

1. A pictorial view of an MP3 music system is shown.
Also shown is a 3D graphic of the music system.

(a) Draw an elevation in the direction of arrow **A**.

(b) Project a plan from the elevation.

(c) Project an end view in the direction of arrow **B**.

(d) Determine the true shape of surface **S**.

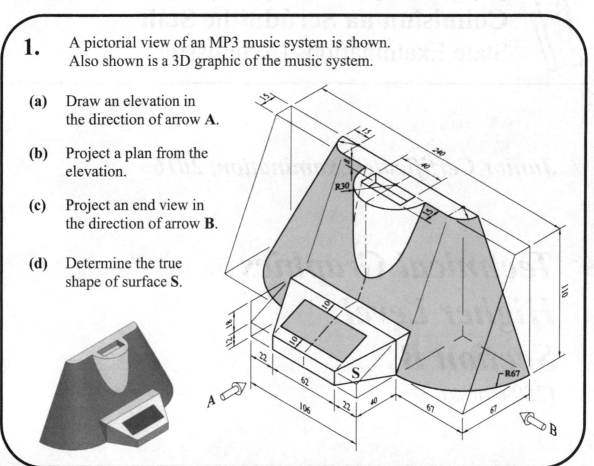

2. The elevation, plan and a 3D graphic of entrance gates to a sports ground are shown. The logo on the gates is based on a regular pentagon **ABCDE** and a circle.

(a) Draw the given elevation and plan.

The gates are opened separately, one through 30° about point **O**, and the other through 45° about point **N**, as shown by the broken lines in plan.

(b) Project an end view of the gates in the direction of arrow **A** to show the gates in their rotated positions.

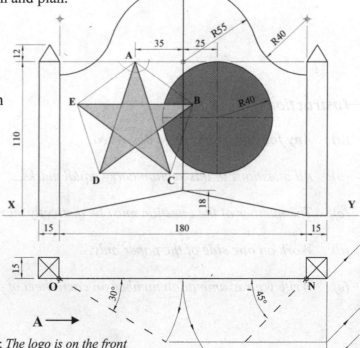

Note: The logo is on the front surface of the gates only.

3. The axonometric axes required for the isometric projection of a torch are shown. The elevation, end-view and a 3D graphic of the torch are also shown.

(a)

(i) Draw the axonometric axes as shown.

(ii) Draw the given elevation inclined at 15° as shown.

(iii) Draw the given end view inclined at 15° as shown.

(iv) Draw the completed axonometric projection of the torch.

OR

(b) Draw the isometric projection of the torch using the isometric scale method.

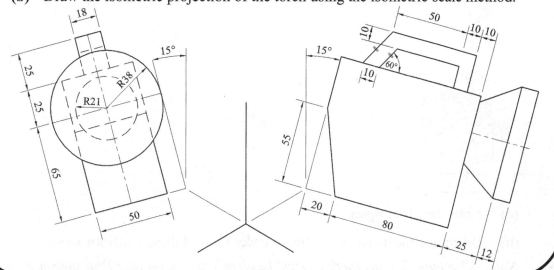

4. The elevation and plan of a safety guard for a garden strimmer are shown. The safety guard consists of a truncated semi-cone **A** and a cylinder **B**, which is also truncated as shown.

A 3D graphic of the guard is also shown.

(a) Draw the given plan and elevation.

(b) Project an end view in the direction of arrow **P**.

(c) Draw the development of the conical surface **A**.

(d) Draw the development of the cylindrical surface **B**.

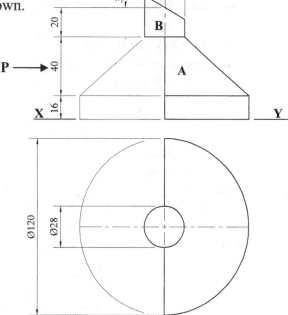

5. The figure shows the design of a video game character.
The shape is subject to transformations in the following order:

- Translation
- Axial Symmetry
- Central Symmetry
- Rotation clockwise through 90°.

P_1, P_2, P_3 and P_4 show the positions of point P under each of these transformations.

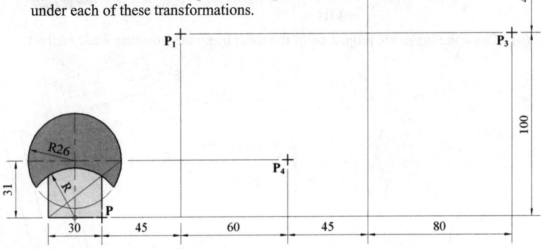

(a) Draw the given figure.

(b) Determine the image of the figure under **each** of these transformations.

Note: All geometric constructions must be clearly shown on your drawing sheet.

6. The figure shows the design for a child's piggy bank.
The curve **ABCDE** is an ellipse and point **B** is a point on the curve.
Determine the length of the major axis and draw the ellipse.
The curve **KMN** is a parabola with vertex at **M**.

The lines **PQ** and **RS** are tangents to the ellipse from points **P** and **R**.

Draw the given design showing clearly all constructions. and points of contact.

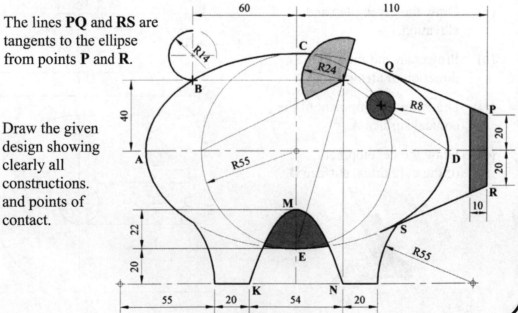

40

Coimisiún na Scrúduithe Stáit
State Examinations Commission

Junior Certificate Examination, 2015

Technical Graphics
Higher Level
Section A
(120 marks)

Monday, 15 June
Morning, 9:30 - 12:30

Centre Number

Instructions

(a)   Answer **any ten** questions in the spaces provided. All questions carry equal marks.

(b)   Construction lines must be clearly shown.

(c)   All measurements are in millimetres.

(d)   This booklet must be handed up at the end of the examination.

(e)   Write your examination number in the box provided below and on all other pages used.

Examination Number:

Question	Mark
Section A	
1	
2	
3	
4	
5	
6	
TOTAL	
GRADE	

SECTION A. Answer **any ten** questions. All questions carry equal marks.

1. Fill in the label for **each** truncated solid by selecting from the given list.

- Triangular Prism
- Cylinder
- Cone
- Pyramid

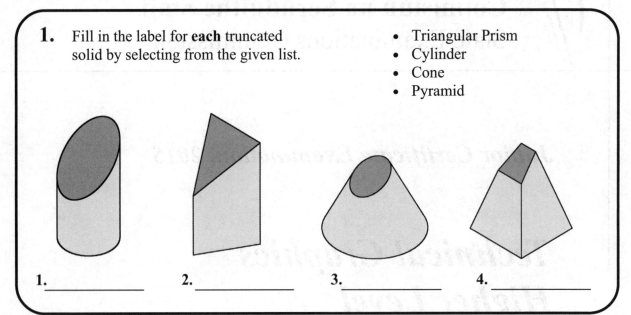

1. _____ 2. _____ 3. _____ 4. _____

2. The figure shows the incomplete perspective drawing of an information stand. A 3D graphic is also shown. Complete the perspective drawing.

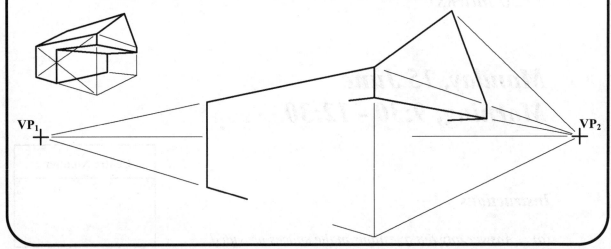

VP₁   VP₂

3. **Fig 1.** shows the logo for a dance school. The logo is composed of polygons and a circle as shown.

Write down the measures of the angles marked **A**, **B** and **C**.

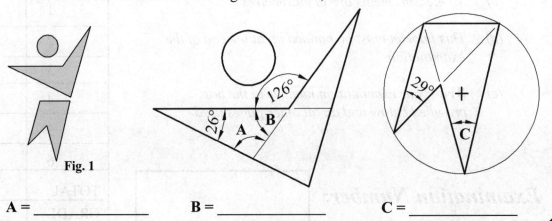

Fig. 1

A = _____   B = _____   C = _____

42

4. The elevation and plan of a sprinter's starting block are shown on the square grid. Make a **freehand pictorial sketch** of the block. Colour **or** shade the sketch.

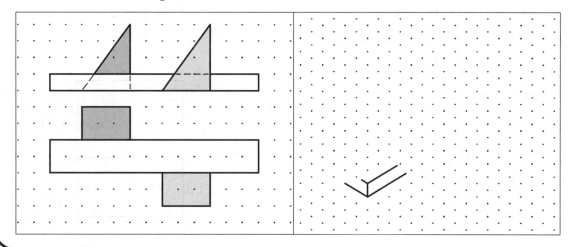

5. The elevation, plan and incomplete development of a dog bed are shown. A 3D graphic of the bed is also shown.

Complete the surface development of the dog bed at **A**.

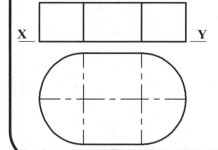

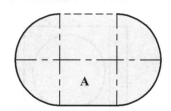

6. The figure shows an isometric projection of a stool drawn using the axonometric axes method. A plan positioned relative to the axes is also shown.

Complete the elevation of the stool in the correct position.

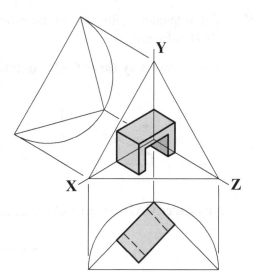

7. The figure shows the elevation and plan of a LUAS tram carriage. A 3D graphic of the carriage is also shown.

Project an auxiliary elevation of the tram carriage on the line X_1-Y_1 to show the true shape of the surface **S**.

8. The elevation and plan of a scientific scales are shown.

In the space provided, draw a **freehand pictorial sketch** of the scales.

Colour **or** shade the sketch.

9. The sequence below shows the process of drawing a stand for a tablet computer using CAD software.

Write down **any three** CAD commands used in the sequence.

Any **three** CAD commands: _____

_____

_____

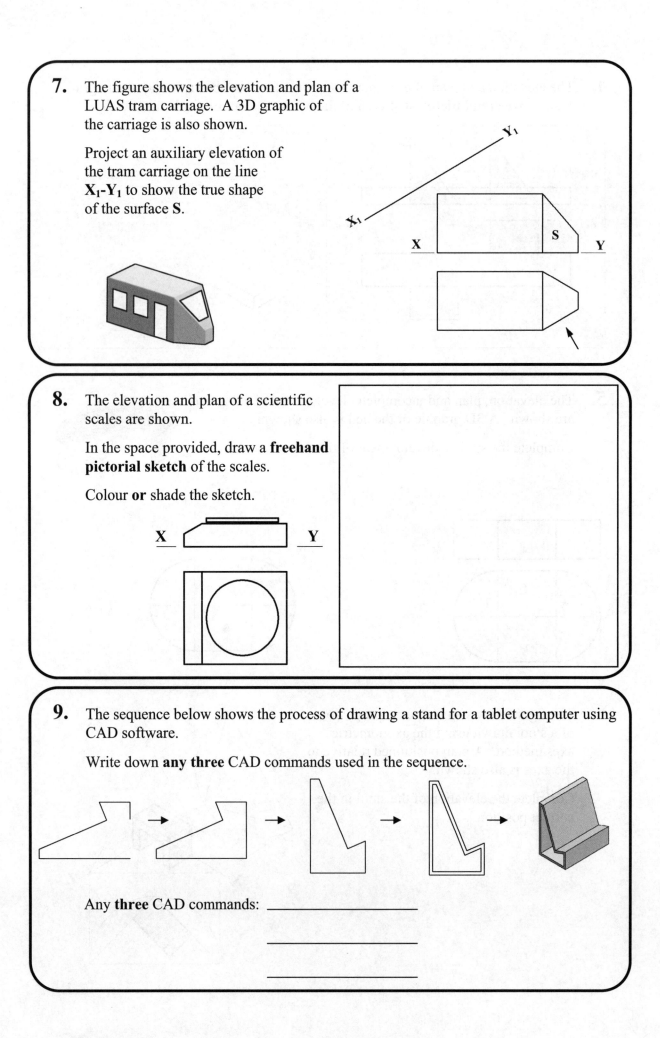

10. The figure shows the elevation of a wheelbarrow.
A 3D graphic of the wheelbarrow is also shown.

Rotate the shaded body of the wheelbarrow **ABCD** about point **O**
until point **A** reaches the line **GG₁**.

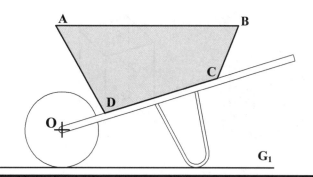

11. **Fig. 1** shows a line of triangular flags. One third of the area of each triangle is
shaded as shown. **Fig. 2** shows the outline of a similar triangular flag.

Divide the area of the flag in **Fig. 2** to show the shaded portion.

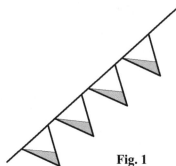

Fig. 1

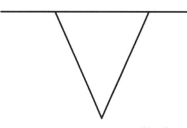

Fig. 2

12. The graphic below shows three sets of children's blocks.
The plan of each set of blocks is shown on the right.

Match the correct letter with the appropriate graphic below.

A

B

C

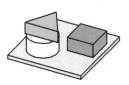

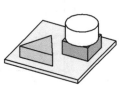

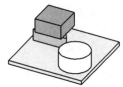

1. _____   2. _____   3. _____

45

13. The graphic shows three solids. Light is shining on the solids, as shown by the direction of the arrow. The shadow cast by the first solid has been completed.

Draw **freehand sketches** of the shadows cast by the other two solids.

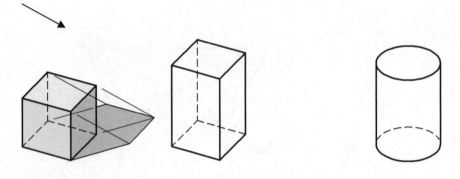

14. **Fig. 1** shows a design for a lounge chair. **Fig. 2** shows the outline of a similar chair.

Complete the outline of the chair in **Fig. 2** by constructing a parabola in the rectangle **ABCD** with its vertex at **E**.

Fig. 1

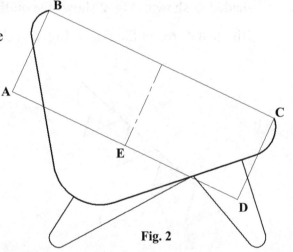

Fig. 2

15. Six county teams competed in a football tournament. Shown below are the number of goals scored by each team during the tournament.

Carlow	-	4 goals
Cavan	-	5 goals
Cork	-	9 goals
Dublin	-	3 goals
Limerick	-	8 goals
Mayo	-	6 goals

Complete the bar chart to represent this information graphically.

Colour **or** shade the completed chart.

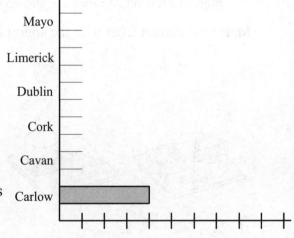

Coimisiún na Scrúduithe Stáit
State Examinations Commission

Junior Certificate Examination, 2015

Technical Graphics
Higher Level
Section B
(280 marks)

2015 HL

Monday, 15 June
Morning, 9:30 - 12:30

Instructions

(a) **Any four** questions to be answered.

(b) All questions in this section carry equal marks.

(c) The number of the question must be distinctly marked by the side of each answer.

(d) Work on **one side** of the paper only.

(e) Write your examination number on each sheet of paper used.

SECTION B.   Answer any **four** questions. All questions carry equal marks.

1. A pictorial view of a concert stage is shown.

(a) Draw an elevation in the direction of arrow **A**.

(b) Project a plan from the elevation.

(c) Project an end view in the direction of arrow **B**.

(d) Determine the true shape of surface **S**.

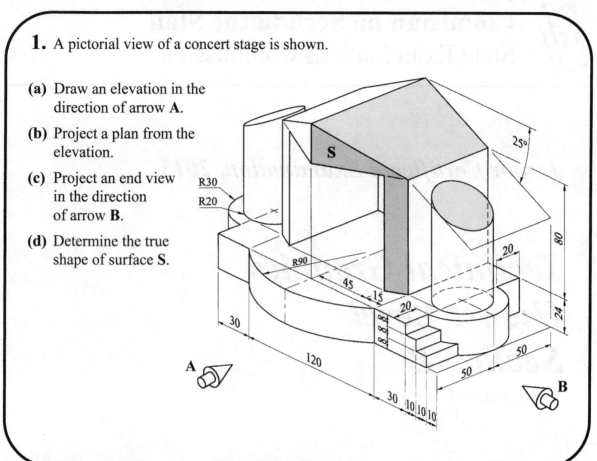

2. The elevation, end view and a 3D graphic of a sign for a fish-shop are shown. The sign is based on a regular hexagon **ABCDEF** and an equilateral triangle **DGH**.

(a) Draw the given elevation and end view.

The sign is rotated through 45° about the point **O** as shown by the broken line in end view.

(b) Project a plan to show the sign in the rotated position.

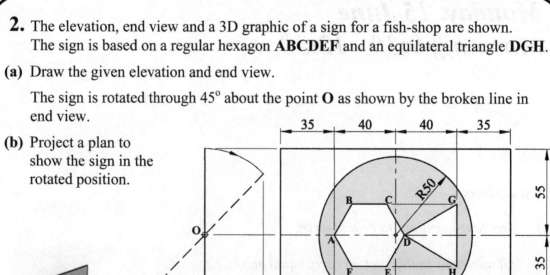

48

3. The axonometric axes required for the isometric projection of a sewing machine are shown. The elevation, end view and a 3D graphic of the sewing machine are also shown.

(a)

(i) Draw the axonometric axes as shown.

(ii) Draw the given elevation inclined at 15° as shown.

(iii) Draw the given end view inclined at 15° as shown.

(iv) Draw the completed axonometric projection of the sewing machine.

OR

(b) Draw the isometric projection of the sewing machine using the isometric scale method.

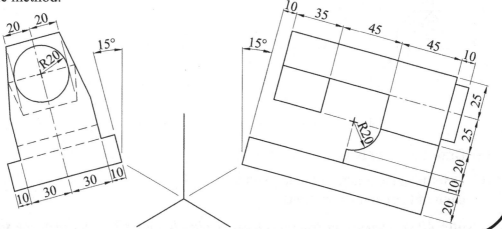

---

4. The elevation and plan of the design for a child's high chair are shown. The high chair consists of a truncated cone **A** and a cylinder **B**, which is truncated as shown.

Also shown is a 3D graphic of the high chair.

(a) Draw the elevation and plan as shown.

(b) Project an end view in the direction of arrow **P**.

(c) Draw the development of the conical surface **A**.

(d) Draw the development of the cylindrical surface **B**.

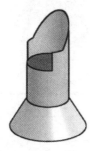

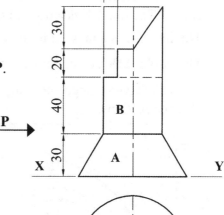

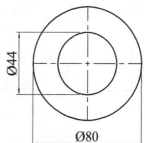

5. The logo for a fitness club is based on a square grid, as shown.
The logo is subject to transformations in the following order:
- Axial Symmetry
- Central Symmetry
- Translation
- Rotation clockwise through 120°.

P_1, P_2, P_3 and P_4 show the positions of point **P** under each of these transformations.

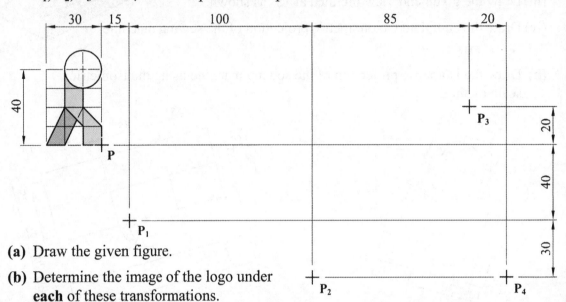

(a) Draw the given figure.

(b) Determine the image of the logo under **each** of these transformations.

Note: *All geometric constructions must be clearly shown on your drawing sheet.*

6. The figure shows a design for a scooter.

The curve **ABC** is a portion of an ellipse with semi-minor axis **CD**. The figure shows the location of the axes and the focal points, F_1 and F_2, of the elliptical curve. The line **BE** is a normal to the ellipse.

The line **CG** is a tangent to the circle from **C**.

The curve **HJK** is a parabola with vertex at **J**.

Draw the given design showing clearly all constructions.

50

Coimisiún na Scrúduithe Stáit
State Examinations Commission

Junior Certificate Examination, 2014

Technical Graphics
Higher Level
Section A
(120 marks)

Monday, 16 June
Morning 9:30 - 12:30

2014 HL

Centre Number

Instructions

(a) Answer **any ten** questions in the spaces provided. All questions carry equal marks.

(b) Construction lines must be clearly shown.

(c) All measurements are in millimetres.

(d) This booklet must be handed up at the end of the examination.

(e) Write your examination number in the box provided below and on all other pages used.

Examination Number:

Question	Mark
Section A	
1	
2	
3	
4	
5	
6	
TOTAL	
GRADE	

SECTION A. Answer **any ten** questions. All questions carry equal marks.

1. Fill in the label for **each** diagram by selecting from the given list.
   - Trapezium
   - Rhombus
   - Parallelogram
   - Rectangle

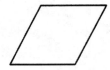 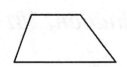 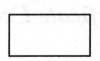 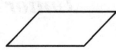

1._____   2._____   3._____   4._____

2. The figure shows the incomplete perspective drawing of a chicken coop. A 3D graphic is also shown. Complete the perspective drawing.

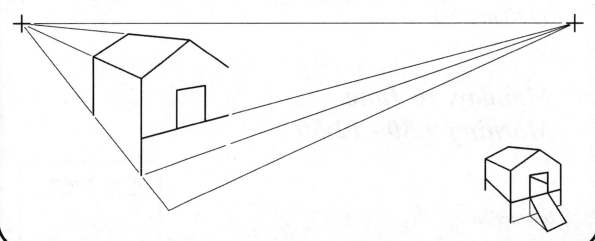

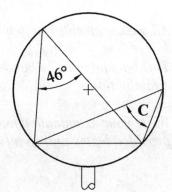

3. Write down the measures of the angles marked **A**, **B** and **C**.

Regular pentagon

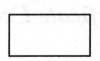

A = _____   B = _____   C = _____

4. The projections of a swimmer's starting block are shown on the square grid.
Make a **freehand pictorial sketch** of the starting block. Colour **or** shade the sketch.

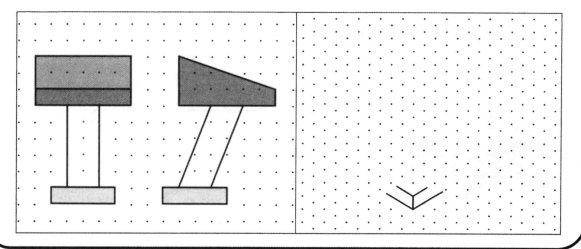

5. The figure shows the end view of a swing seat.
Also shown is a 3D graphic of the seat.

Rotate the seat about point **L**
until point **P** reaches the line **LL₁**.

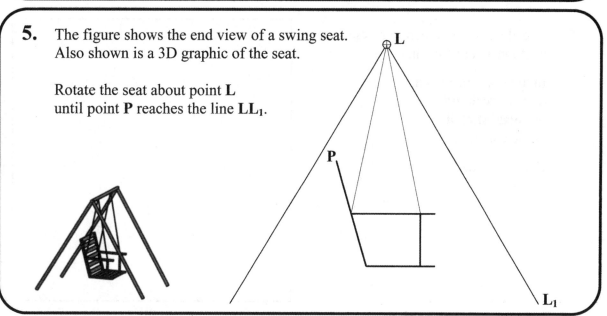

6. The figure shows the axonometric axes
required to draw an isometric view.
Also shown is the position of the plan.

Complete the construction to show the
position of the elevation.

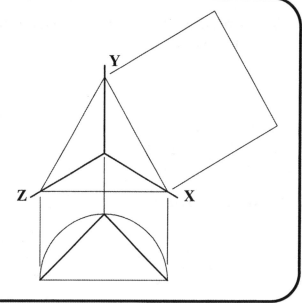

7. The figure shows the elevation and plan of a stage light. A 3D graphic is also shown.

Project an auxiliary elevation of the stage light on the line X_1-Y_1 to show the true shape of the surface **S**.

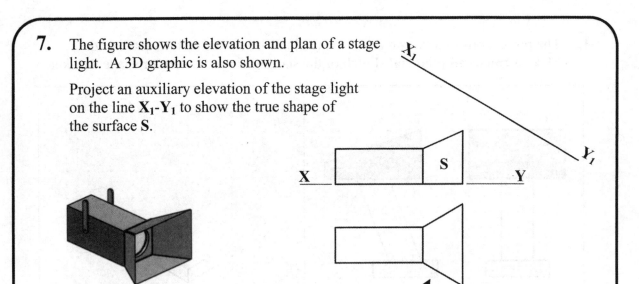

8. The elevation and plan of an electronic component are shown.

In the space provided, draw a **freehand pictorial sketch** of the component.

Colour **or** shade the sketch.

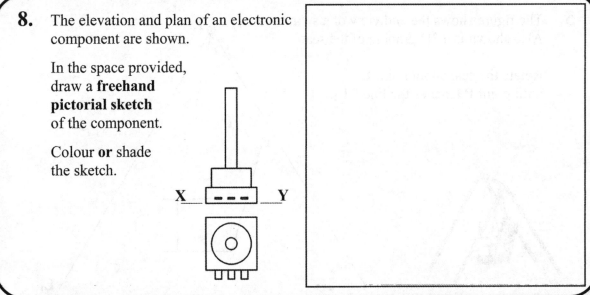

9. Write down **any three** CAD commands used to edit the clock-case as shown in the sequence below.

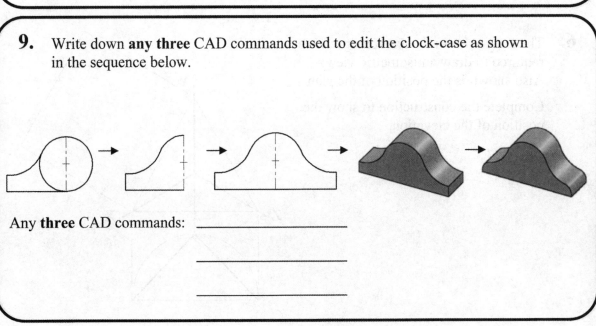

Any **three** CAD commands: _____

_____

_____

10. The 3D graphic shows a child's rocker. The base of the rocker is a semi-ellipse. The figure shows the location of the axes and focal points of the semi-ellipse.

P is a point on the curve. Determine the lengths of the major and minor axes and draw the semi-ellipse.

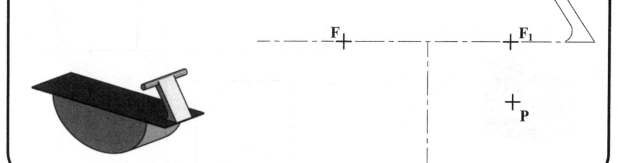

11. **Fig. 1** shows a design for an alloy wheel. **Fig. 2** shows the outline an identical wheel. Determine the centre of the wheel in **Fig. 2**.

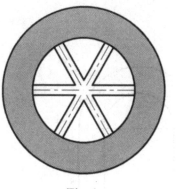

Fig. 1

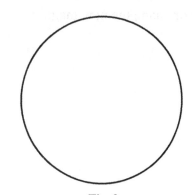

Fig. 2

12. Draw **two** axes of symmetry on the figure shown.

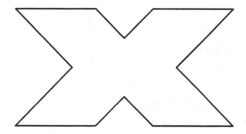

13. The figure shows the plan and end view of a clothes bank. A 3D graphic of the clothes bank is also shown. Project the elevation of the clothes bank.

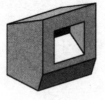

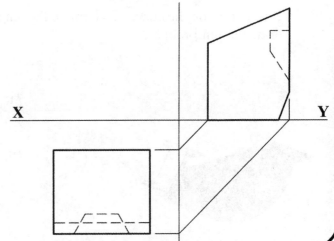

X ———————————————— Y

14. The figure shows the outline of a magnet.

Draw a new magnet similar to the given magnet, with length **AB** increased to **AB₁**.

Colour **or** shade the new magnet.

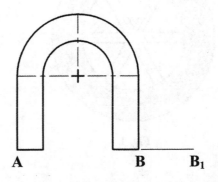

A   B   B₁

15. A 3rd year student was asked to present her daily routine for a typical school day.

The result was as follows:

Sleep/Rest	-	12 hours
School	-	6 hours
Study	-	4 hours
Leisure	-	2 hours

Divide the given circle to represent this information graphically as a pie chart.

Colour **or** shade the completed pie chart.

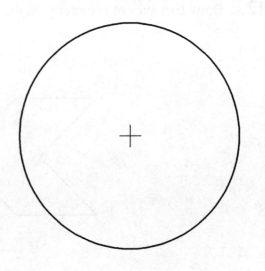

Coimisiún na Scrúduithe Stáit
State Examinations Commission

Junior Certificate Examination, 2014

Technical Graphics
Higher Level
Section B
(280 marks)

Monday, 16 June
Morning 9:30 - 12:30

Instructions

*(a) **Any four** questions to be answered.*

(b) All questions in this section carry equal marks.

(c) The number of the question must be distinctly marked by the side of each answer.

*(d) Work on **one side** of the paper only.*

(e) Write your examination number on each sheet of paper used.

SECTION B. Answer any **four** questions. All questions carry equal marks.

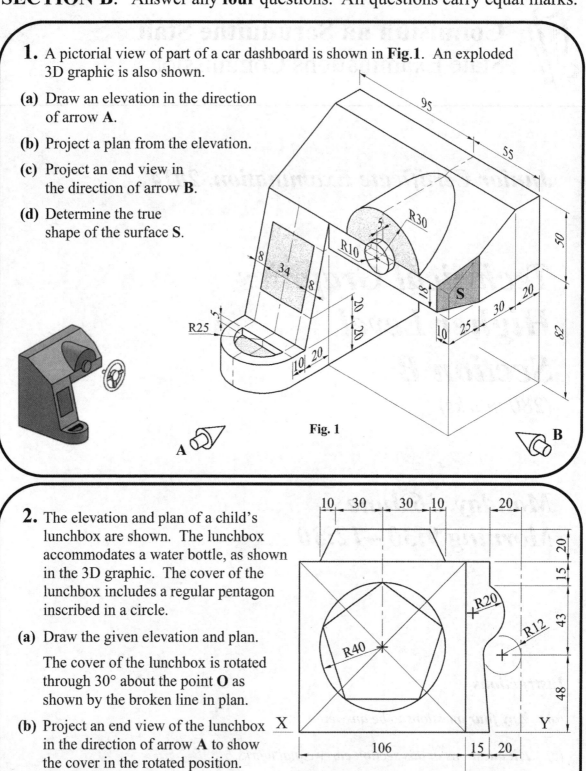

1. A pictorial view of part of a car dashboard is shown in **Fig.1**. An exploded 3D graphic is also shown.

(a) Draw an elevation in the direction of arrow **A**.

(b) Project a plan from the elevation.

(c) Project an end view in the direction of arrow **B**.

(d) Determine the true shape of the surface **S**.

Fig. 1

2. The elevation and plan of a child's lunchbox are shown. The lunchbox accommodates a water bottle, as shown in the 3D graphic. The cover of the lunchbox includes a regular pentagon inscribed in a circle.

(a) Draw the given elevation and plan.

The cover of the lunchbox is rotated through 30° about the point **O** as shown by the broken line in plan.

(b) Project an end view of the lunchbox in the direction of arrow **A** to show the cover in the rotated position.

58

3. The axonometric axes required for the isometric projection of a toy truck are shown. The elevation, end view and a 3D graphic of the truck are also shown.

(a)

(i) Draw the axonometric axes as shown.

(ii) Draw the given elevation inclined at 15° as shown.

(iii) Draw the given end view inclined at 15° as shown.

(iv) Draw the completed axonometric projection of the toy truck.

OR

(b) Draw the isometric projection of the toy truck using the isometric scale method.

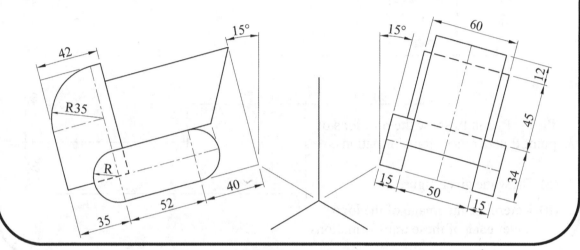

4. The elevation and plan of a set of science equipment are shown. A 3D graphic of the equipment is also shown.

(a) Draw the given elevation and plan, showing all constructions.

(b) Draw the development of the conical surface **A**.

(c) Show all points of contact.

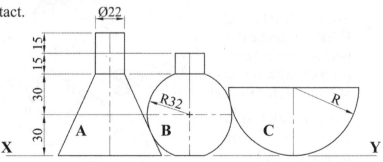

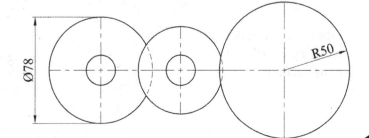

5. The figure shows the logo of a music app for a smartphone.
The logo is subject to transformations in the following order:
- Central Symmetry
- Translation
- Axial Symmetry
- Rotation clockwise through 90°.

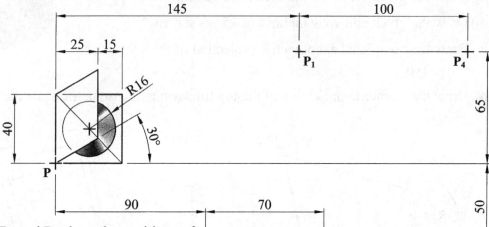

P_1, P_2, P_3 and P_4 show the positions of point **P** under these transformations.

(a) Draw the given figure.

(b) Determine the image of the logo under **each** of these transformations.

6. The figure shows a logo for an animal shelter.

The curve **ABC** is a parabola with vertex at **B**.

The curves **DEF** and **GHF** are identical to portions of the same parabola with vertices at **E** and **H**, respectively.

The curve **JKLM** is an ellipse with focal points at **N** and **P**.

Draw the given design showing clearly all construction.

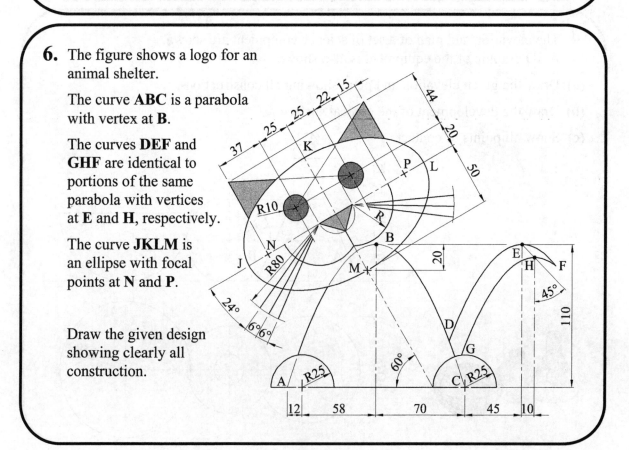

60

Coimisiún na Scrúduithe Stáit
State Examinations Commission

Junior Certificate Examination, 2013

Technical Graphics
Higher Level
Section A
(120 marks)

Monday, 17 June
Morning 9:30 - 12:30

Centre Number

Instructions

*(a)   Answer **any ten** questions in the spaces provided. All questions carry equal marks.*

(b)   Construction lines must be clearly shown.

(c)   All measurements are in millimetres.

(d)   This booklet must be handed up at the end of the examination.

(e)   Write your examination number in the box provided below and on all other pages used.

Question	Mark
Section A	
1	
2	
3	
4	
5	
6	
TOTAL	
GRADE	

Examination Number:

2013 HL

SECTION A. Answer **any ten** questions. All questions carry equal marks.

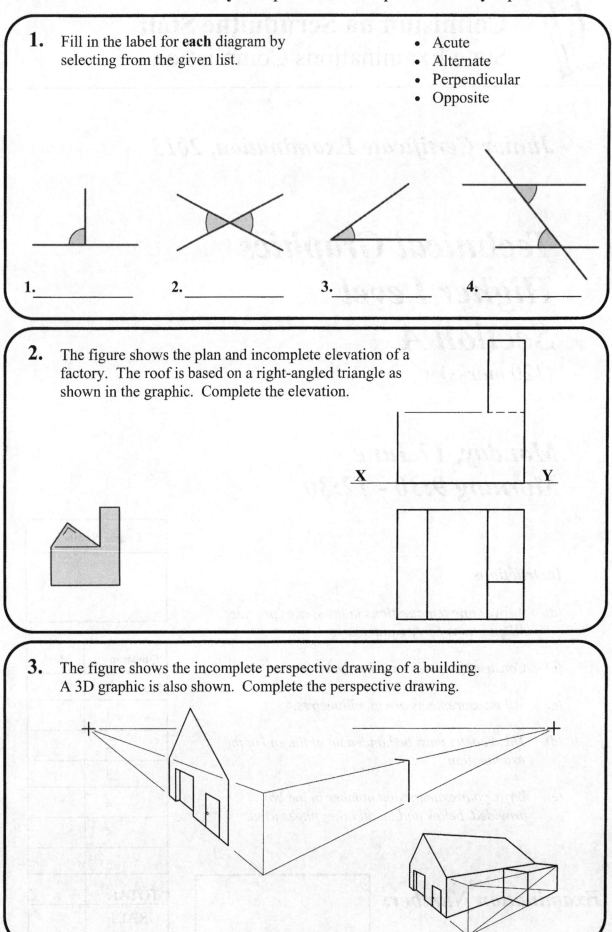

1. Fill in the label for **each** diagram by selecting from the given list.

- Acute
- Alternate
- Perpendicular
- Opposite

1._____

2._____

3._____

4._____

2. The figure shows the plan and incomplete elevation of a factory. The roof is based on a right-angled triangle as shown in the graphic. Complete the elevation.

X   Y

3. The figure shows the incomplete perspective drawing of a building. A 3D graphic is also shown. Complete the perspective drawing.

4. The elevation and end view of a chair are shown on the square grid.
Make a **freehand pictorial sketch** of the chair. Colour **or** shade the sketch.

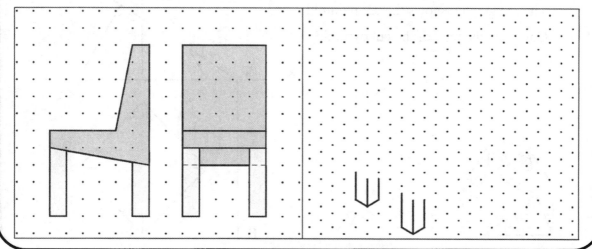

5. The graphic shows an advertisement on a newspaper page. **Fig. 1** shows a triangle that represents the area of the advertisement. Convert the triangle to a rectangle of equal area to show the final size of the advertisement.

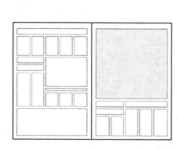

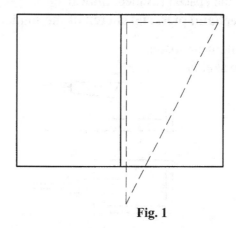

Fig. 1

6. The 3D graphic shows a playground feature. The top of the feature is based on a semi-ellipse. The figure below shows the location of the axes and focal points of the semi-ellipse. The point **P** is a point on the curve.
Find the length of the major and minor axes and draw the semi-ellipse.

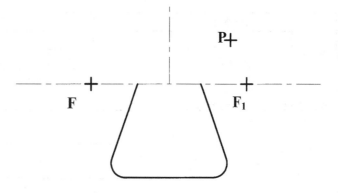

7. The figure shows the elevation and plan of a pyramid which is cut by the plane **VTH**.
The 3D graphic shows the cut pyramid.

Complete the plan of the cut pyramid.

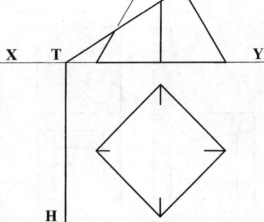

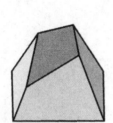

8. The elevation and plan of an orbital sander are shown.

In the space provided, draw a **freehand pictorial sketch** of the sander.

Colour **or** shade the sketch.

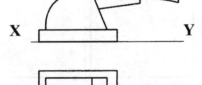

9. Write down **any three** CAD commands used to edit the figure as shown in the sequence.

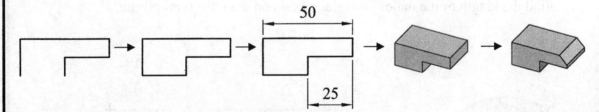

Any **three** CAD commands: _____

_____

_____

10. The figure shows the plan and end view of a soap dispenser. A 3D graphic of the dispenser is also shown. Project the elevation of the dispenser.

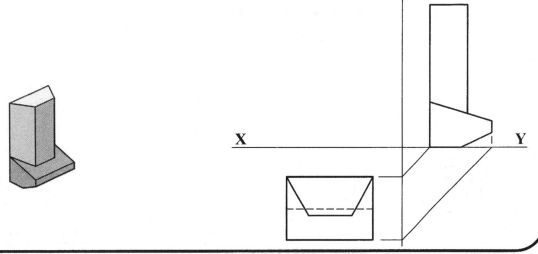

11. The figure shows a tower crane.
Write down the measures of the angles **A**, **B** and **C**.

A = _____

B = _____

C = _____

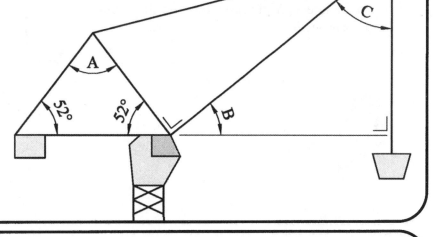

12. The graphic shows a logo based on a racing car. **Fig. 1** shows the incomplete logo. Complete the logo by drawing a tangent between the wheels of the car. Show all construction and points of contact.

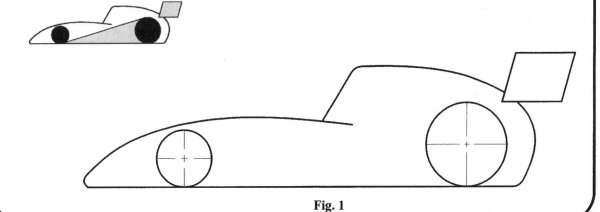

Fig. 1

13. The 3D graphic shows a plate rack. Also shown is an elevation of the plate rack and a plate. Draw the plate in position on the plate rack. Show all construction and points of contact.

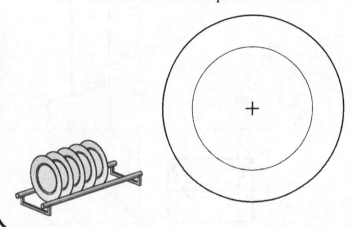

14. The figure shows the elevation and plan of a knife block. A 3D graphic of the knife block is also shown.

Project an auxiliary elevation of the knife block on the line X_1-Y_1 to show the true shape of the surface **S**.

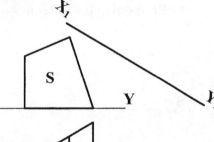

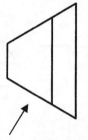

15. The **X** and **Y** axes shown are marked in single-unit intervals.

Complete the graph using the following coordinates:

A - (-1,1)
B - (1,5)
C - (3,2)
D - (5,0)
E - (6,1)
F - (8,6)

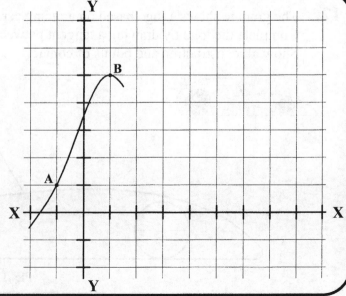

Coimisiún na Scrúduithe Stáit
State Examinations Commission

Junior Certificate Examination, 2013

Technical Graphics
Higher Level
Section B
(280 marks)

Monday, 17 June
Morning 9:30 - 12:30

Instructions

(a)   Answer **any four** questions.

(b)   All questions in this section carry equal marks.

(c)   The number of the question must be distinctly marked by the side of each answer.

(d)   Work on **one side** of the paper only.

(e)   Write your examination number on each sheet of paper used.

1. A pictorial view of a drinks machine is shown.
A 3D graphic of the drinks machine is also shown.

(a) Draw an elevation
in the direction of
arrow **A**.

(b) Project a plan from
the elevation.

(c) Project an end view
in the direction of
arrow **B**.

(d) Determine the true
shape of surface **S**.

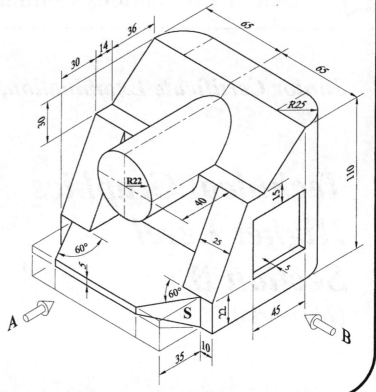

2. The elevation, plan and a 3D graphic
of a child's walker are shown.

The design of the walker includes
holes in the shape of a square, an
equilateral triangle and a regular
pentagon.

(a) Draw the given plan and elevation.

The lid of the walker is rotated
through 45° about the point **O** as
shown by the broken line in elevation.

(b) Project an end view of the walker
in the direction of arrow **A** to show
the lid in the rotated position.

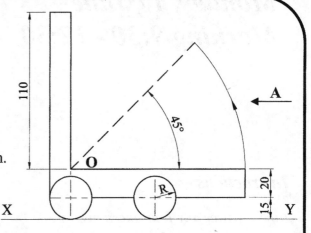

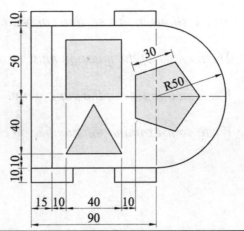

3. The axonometric axes required for the isometric projection of a *half-pipe* from a skateboard park are shown. The elevation, plan and a 3D graphic of the structure are also shown.

(a)

(i) Draw the axonometric axes as shown.

(ii) Draw the given elevation inclined at 15° as shown.

(iii) Draw the given plan inclined at 45° as shown.

(iv) Draw the completed axonometric projection of the half-pipe.

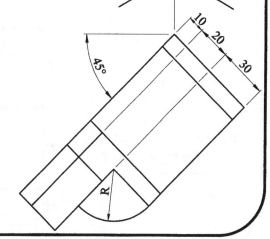

OR

(b) Draw the isometric projection of the half-pipe using the isometric scale method.

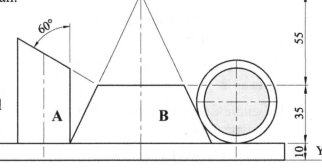

4. The elevation and plan of a desk organiser are shown. A 3D graphic of the desk organiser is also shown.

(a) Draw the given elevation and plan. Show all points of contact.

(b) Draw the development of the cylindrical surface **A**.

(c) Draw the development of the sloping surfaces of the truncated pyramid **B**.

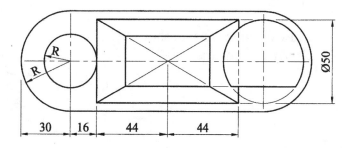

5. The figure shows the logo for a college.

The logo is subject to transformations in the following order:

- Central Symmetry
- Axial Symmetry
- Translation
- Rotation clockwise through 120°.

P_1, P_2, P_3 and P_4 show the positions of point **P** under each of these transformations.

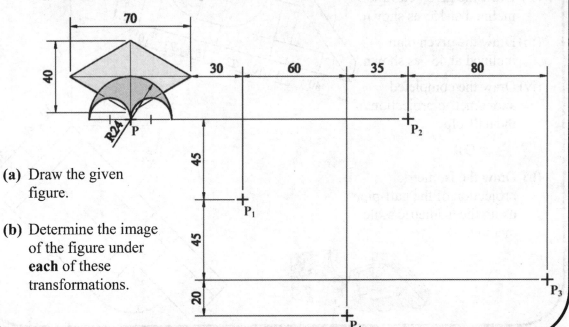

(a) Draw the given figure.

(b) Determine the image of the figure under **each** of these transformations.

6. The figure shows a design for a toy rocket.

The curve **BCDEG** is a semi-ellipse.

The curve **LMN** is identical to a portion of the same ellipse.

The curve **BA** is a parabola with the vertex at **B**.

The curve **GA** is an identical parabola with vertex at **G**.

The lines **CJ** and **EK** are tangents to the ellipse.

Draw the given design showing clearly all constructions.

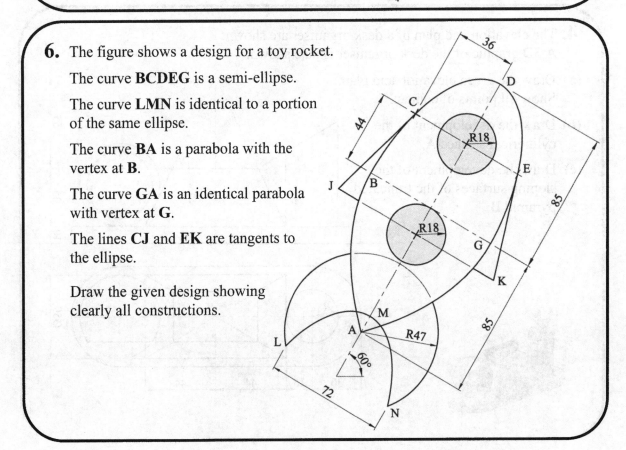

70

Coimisiún na Scrúduithe Stáit
State Examinations Commission

Junior Certificate Examination, 2012

Technical Graphics
Higher Level
Section A
(120 marks)

Monday, 18 June
Morning 9:30 - 12:30

Centre Number

Instructions

(a) Answer **any ten** questions in the spaces provided. All questions carry equal marks.

(b) Construction lines must be clearly shown.

(c) All measurements are in millimetres.

(d) This booklet must be handed up at the end of the examination.

(e) Write your examination number in the box provided below and on all other pages used.

Question	Mark
Section A	
1	
2	
3	
4	
5	
6	
TOTAL	
GRADE	

2012 HL

Examination Number: [ ]

SECTION A. Answer **any ten** questions. All questions carry equal marks.

1   Fill in the label for **each** diagram by selecting from the projections given in the list.

Projection:
- Orthographic
- Isometric
- Oblique
- Planometric

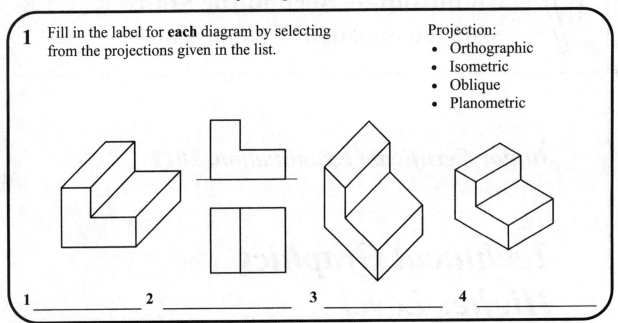

1 _____   2 _____   3 _____   4 _____

2   The incomplete elevation of a lounger chair is shown. A 3D graphic of the chair is also shown. Complete the elevation by drawing the arc **BC**.

The arc **BC** has a radius of 35 mm and is tangential to the arc **AB**.

Show the point of contact between the arcs.

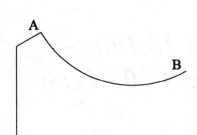

3   The figure shows the perspective drawing of a bouncy castle. The drawing is not complete. A 3D graphic of the bouncy castle is also shown.
Complete the perspective drawing.

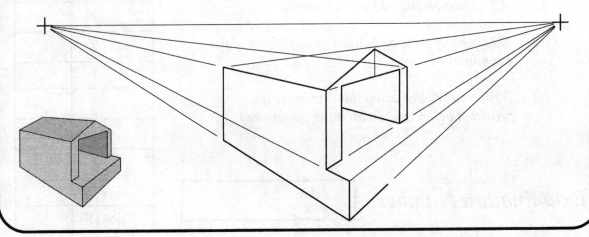

72

4 The elevation and end view of a workbench are shown.
Make a **freehand pictorial sketch** of the workbench. Colour **or** shade the sketch.

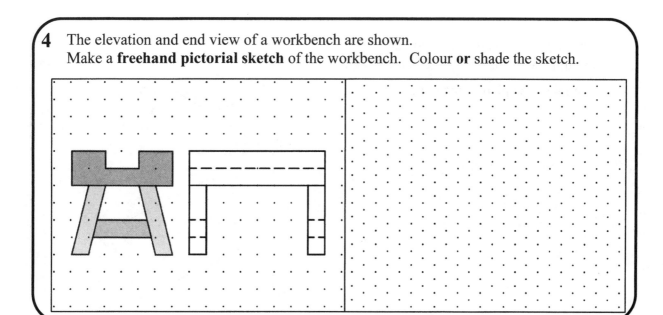

5 The figure shows the elevation and end view of a sports net.
A 3D graphic of the net is also shown. Draw a development of the sports net.

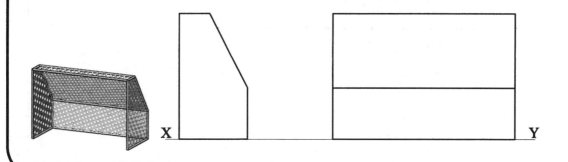

6 The 3D graphic shows a reflective road safety sign with panels of equal width.
Complete the elevation of the sign showing clearly how to determine the width of the panels.

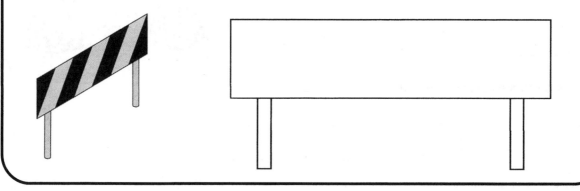

7 The figure shows the elevation and plan of a pyramid which is cut by the plane **VTH**.

Complete the plan of the pyramid.

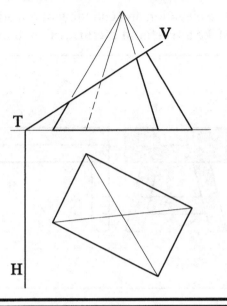

8 The elevation and plan of a kicking tee are shown. In the space provided, draw a **freehand pictorial sketch** of the kicking tee.

Colour **or** shade the sketch.

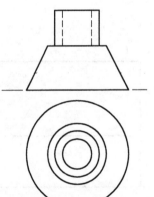

9 Write down **any three** CAD commands used to edit the figure as shown in the sequence.

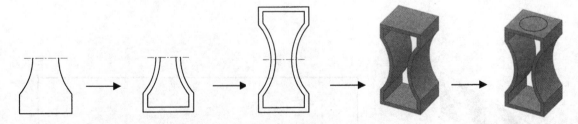

Any **three** CAD commands: _____

_____

_____

10 The figure shows the elevation of an entrance barrier. Also shown is a 3D graphic of the barrier in the closed position.

Rotate the barrier about point **P** to show the barrier in the open position, as indicated by the broken line.

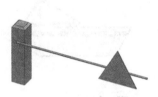
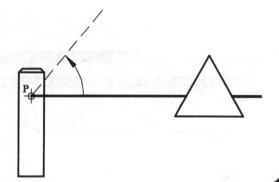

11 Write down the measure of the angles **A, B** and **C**.

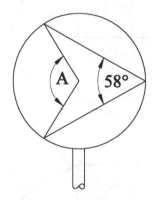

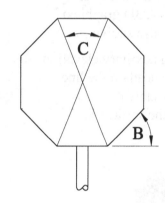

A = _____   B = _____   C = _____

12 **Fig. 1** shows the triangle **ABC** inscribed in a semi-ellipse. **Fig. 2** shows the axes and focal points of the ellipse and a point **P** on the curve. Determine the length of the major and minor axes and draw the triangle **ABC** in **Fig. 2**.

Note: It is not necessary to draw the semi-ellipse.

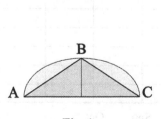

Fig. 1   Fig. 2

13 **Fig. 1** shows the design of a model speed boat. The design is not complete.
Fig. 2 shows a small graphic of the boat, including the windscreen. The windscreen is
based on a right-angled triangle. Complete **Fig. 1** to show the windscreen of the boat.

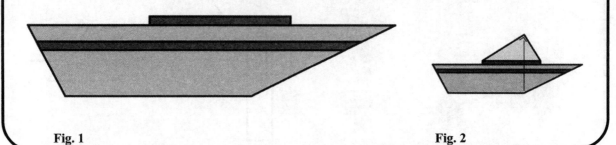

Fig. 1   Fig. 2

14 The figure shows the
elevation and plan of an
axe head. A 3D graphic of
the axe is also shown.

Project an auxiliary elevation
of the axe head on the line
X1-Y1 to show the true
shape of the surface **S**.

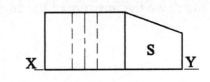

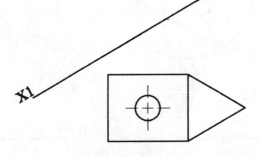

15 Sales of equipment for technical graphics
were recorded during a six month period.
The following were the sales:

- July   -   € 300
- August -   € 500
- Sept   -   € 900
- Oct   -   € 400
- Nov   -   € 300
- Dec   -   € 600

Complete the chart to represent this
information graphically.

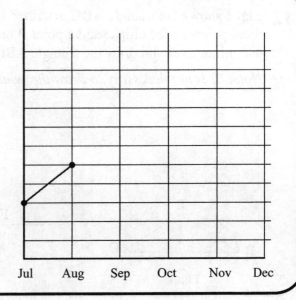

Jul   Aug   Sep   Oct   Nov   Dec

Coimisiún na Scrúduithe Stáit
State Examinations Commission

Junior Certificate Examination, 2012

Technical Graphics
Higher Level
Section B
(280 marks)

Monday, 18 June
Morning 9:30 - 12:30

Instructions

(a) **Any four** questions to be answered.

(b) All questions in this section carry equal marks.

(c) The number of the question must be distinctly marked by the side of each answer.

(d) Work on **one side** of the paper only.

(e) Write your examination number on each sheet of paper used.

2012 HL

SECTION B. Answer any **four** questions. All questions carry equal marks.

1 A pictorial view of the design for a lawnmower is shown. A 3D graphic of the lawnmower is also shown.

(a) Draw an elevation in the direction of arrow **A**.

(b) Project a plan from the elevation.

(c) Project an end view in the direction of arrow **B**.

(d) Determine the true shape of surface **S**.

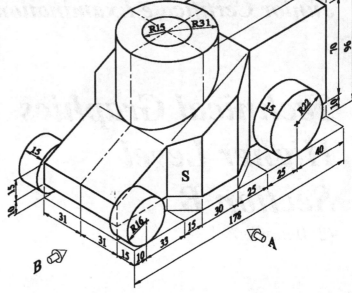

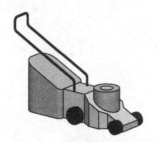

2 The elevation, plan and a 3D graphic of a weather vane are shown. A square is inscribed in the circle as shown. The weather vane is rotated through 30° about point **O**, as shown by the broken line in plan.

(a) Draw the given elevation and plan showing all constructions.

(b) Project an end view of the weather vane in the direction of arrow **A** to show the weather vane in the rotated position.

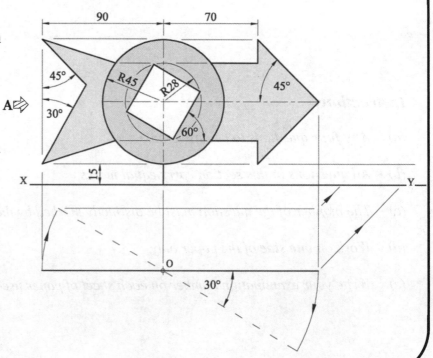

78

3 The axonometric axes required for the isometric projection of an ornamental well are shown. The elevation, plan and a 3D graphic of the well are also shown.

(a)

(i) Draw the axonometric axes as shown.

(ii) Draw the given plan orientated at 45° as shown.

(iii) Draw the given elevation orientated at 15° as shown.

(iv) Draw the completed axonometric projection of the well.

OR

(b) Draw the completed isometric projection of the well using the isometric scale method.

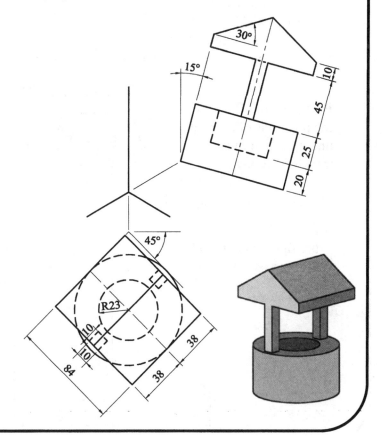

4 The drawing shows the elevation and plan of an arrangement of ceiling lights. A 3D graphic of the lights is also shown.

(a) Draw the given elevation and plan, showing how to obtain the centre of the sphere **C**.

(b) Draw a development of the cylindrical surface **A**.

(c) Draw a development of the conical surface **B**.

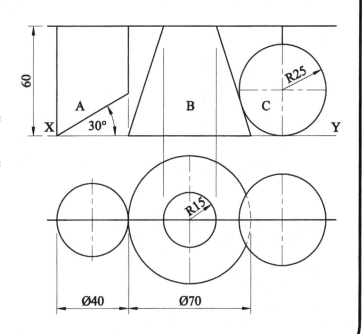

5 The figure shows a logo for an art gallery.
The figure is subject to transformations in the following order:

- Translation
- Axial Symmetry
- Central Symmetry
- Rotation anti-clockwise through 120°.

P₁, P₂, P₃ and **P₄** show the positions of point **P** under each of these transformations.

(a) Draw the given figure.

(b) Determine the image of the figure under **each** of these transformations.

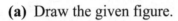
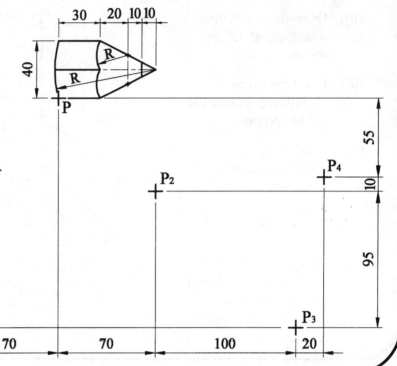

---

6 The figure shows a logo for riding stables.
The curve **AB** is parabolic with vertex at **B**. The curve **TDE** is a portion of an ellipse.
The points **F** and **F1** are the focal points of the ellipse as shown.

The line **BT** is a tangent to the ellipse from **B**.

The curve **LM,** with vertex at **L**, is identical to a portion of the ellipse.

The line **RS** is a tangent to the circle from **S**.

Locate the centre of arc **APS** and draw the arc.

Draw the given logo showing clearly all construction lines and points of contact.

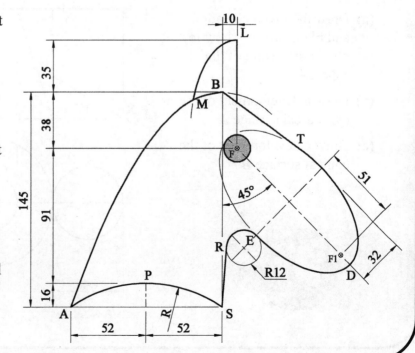

80

Coimisiún na Scrúduithe Stáit
State Examinations Commission

Junior Certificate Examination, 2011

Technical Graphics
Higher Level
Section A
(120 marks)

Monday, 20 June
Morning 9:30 - 12:30

Centre Number

Instructions

(a) Answer **any ten** questions in the spaces provided. All questions carry equal marks.

(b) Construction lines must be clearly shown.

(c) All measurements are in millimetres.

(d) This booklet must be handed up at the end of the examination.

(e) Write your examination number in the box provided below and on all other pages used.

Question	Mark
Section A	
1	
2	
3	
4	
5	
6	
TOTAL	
GRADE	

2011 HL

Examination Number:

SECTION A. Answer **any ten** questions. All questions carry equal marks.

1 Fill in the label for **each** diagram by selecting from the given list.

- Isosceles
- Equilateral
- Right-angled
- Scalene

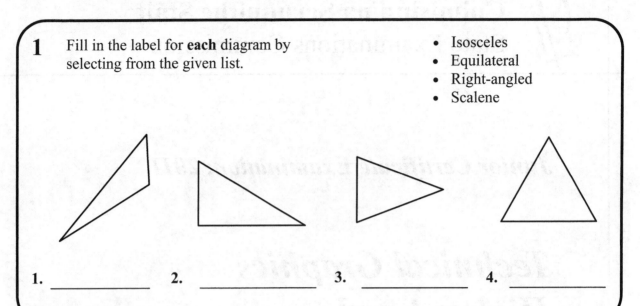

1. _____   2. _____   3. _____   4. _____

2 Complete the elevation of the given sign in its rotated position, as shown by the broken line in plan.

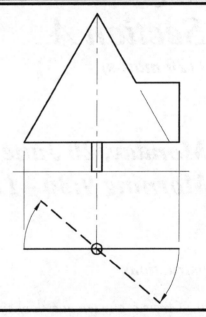

3 The figure shows the incomplete perspective drawing of a building. A small 3D graphic is also shown. Complete the perspective drawing.

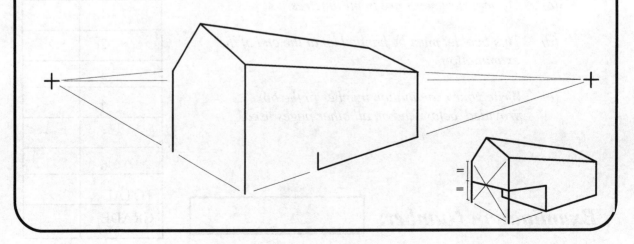

4 The elevation and end view of a fireplace are shown on the square grid.
Make a pictorial sketch of the fireplace. Colour **or** shade the completed sketch.

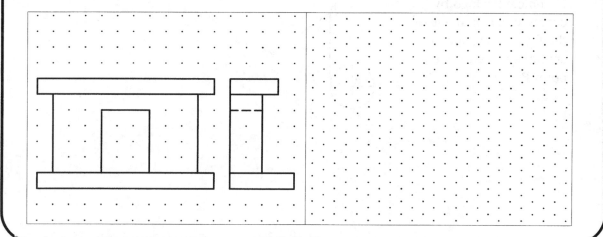

5 The figure shows the outline of a car door and a window **ABCD**.
Draw a triangular window equal in area to the quadrilateral window **ABCD** having a vertex of the triangle at **B**.

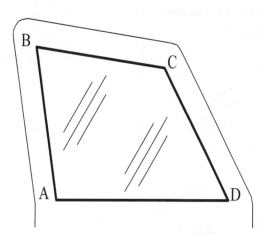

6 A gate with seven panels of equal width is shown in the 3D graphic.
Complete the elevation of the gate showing clearly how to determine the width of the panels.

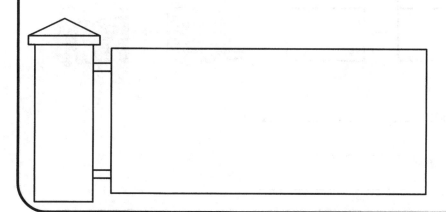

2011 HL

7 The figure shows a logo for a music shop. The logo is not complete.

Complete the logo by constructing an image of the figure **abc** under a central symmetry in the point **P**.

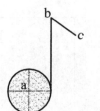

+ P

8 The elevation and plan of a whistle are shown.

In the space provided, draw a **freehand pictorial sketch** of the whistle.

Colour **or** shade the sketch.

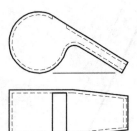

9 Write down **any three** CAD commands used to edit the figure shown in the sequence below.

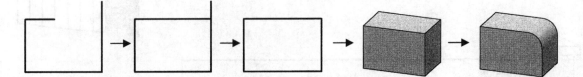

Any **three** CAD commands: _____

_____

_____

10 The figure shows a puzzle made from identical cubes.

Write down the number of cubes in this puzzle.

There are _____ cubes in this puzzle.

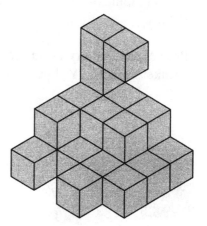

11 Write down the measure of the angles marked **A**, **B** and **C**.

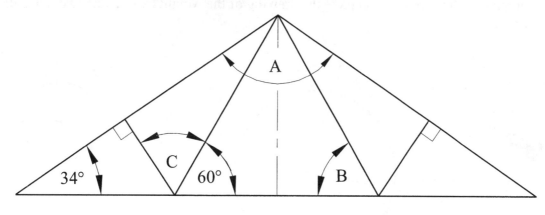

A = _____   B = _____   C = _____

12 The figure shows the design of a remote control car. Also shown is a small graphic of the car and aerial. **AB** is the major axis of the ellipse and the aerial is a normal to the ellipse at **P**. Determine the focal points of the ellipse and draw the aerial at **P**.

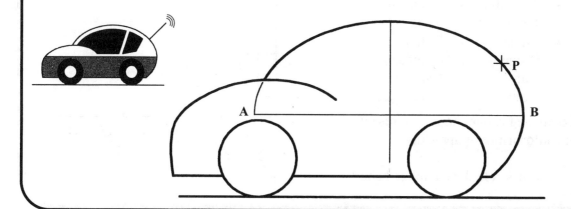

13 The figure shows the elevation and plan of a speaker for an audio system. A 3D graphic of the system is also shown.

Project an auxiliary elevation of the speaker on the X_1Y_1 line shown.

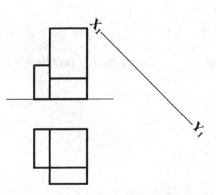

14 The figure shows the incomplete outline of a fishing weight. Also shown is a 3D graphic of the weight. Complete the drawing of the weight by drawing two tangential lines.

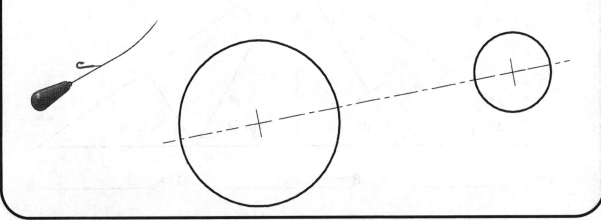

15 Thirty students were surveyed about the musical instruments they play. The following are the results of the survey:

- Accordion - 3 students
- Tin whistle - 5 students
- Guitar - 8 students
- Drums - 6 students
- Piano - 6 students
- Fiddle - 2 students.

Complete the bar chart to represent this information graphically.

Colour **or** shade the completed chart.

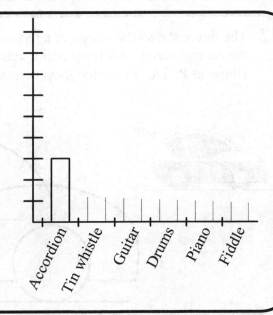

Coimisiún na Scrúduithe Stáit
State Examinations Commission

Junior Certificate Examination, 2011

Technical Graphics
Higher Level
Section B
(280 marks)

Monday, 20 June
Morning 9:30 - 12:30

Instructions

(a) *Any four questions to be answered.*

(b) *All questions in this section carry equal marks.*

(c) *The number of the question must be distinctly marked by the side of each answer.*

(d) *Work on one side of the paper only.*

(e) *Write your examination number on each sheet of paper used.*

2011 HL

SECTION B. Answer any **four** questions. All questions carry equal marks.

1 A pictorial view of a model boat is shown.

(a) Draw an elevation in the direction of arrow **A**.

(b) Project a plan from the elevation.

(c) Project an end view in the direction of arrow **B**.

(d) Determine the true shape of surface **S**.

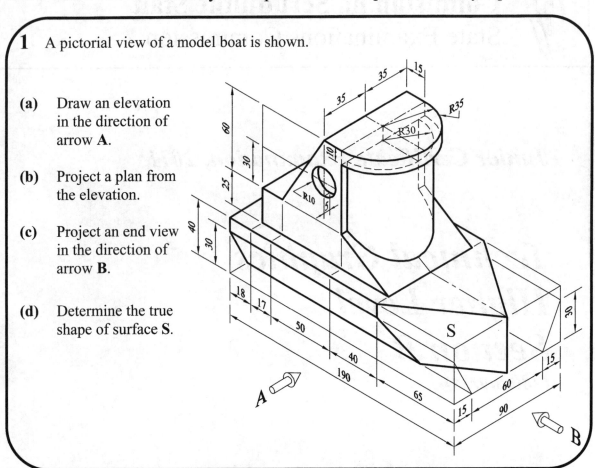

2 The elevation, end view and incomplete plan of the flap of a shoulder bag are shown. Also shown is a 3D graphic of the bag.
The logo on the flap is based on a regular pentagon **ABCDE**, a sector of a circle with centre **E** and a parallelogram **CBFG**.
The flap is rotated through 45° about **L-L**, as shown by the broken line in the end view.

(a) Draw the given elevation and end view.

(b) Project a plan of the flap on **L-L** to show the flap and logo in the rotated position.

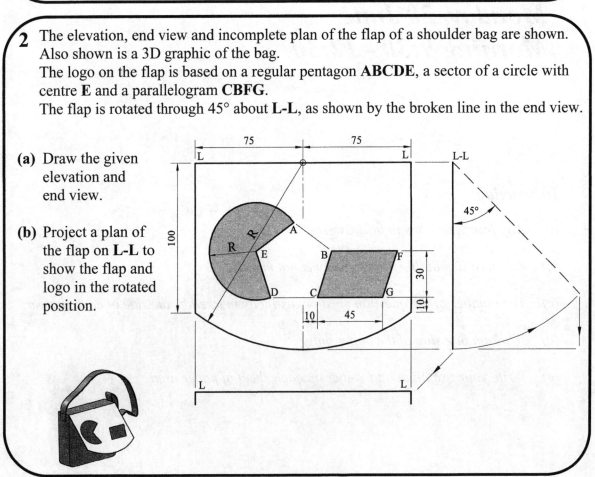

3   The axonometric axes required for the isometric projection of a trolley bag are shown. Also shown is the elevation, plan and a 3D graphic of the trolley bag.

(a)

(i)   Draw the axonometric axes as shown.

(ii) Draw the plan orientated at 45° as shown.

(iii) Draw the elevation orientated at 15° as shown.

(iv) Draw the completed axonometric projection of the trolley bag.

OR

(b) Draw the completed isometric projection of the trolley bag using the isometric scale method.

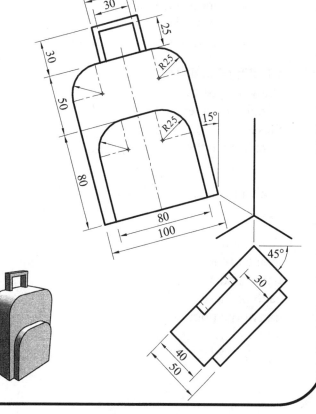

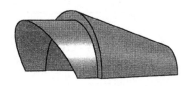

4   The elevation and plan of the design for a small tent are shown. The tent consists of a truncated semi-cone **A** and half a cylinder **B**, which is truncated as shown. Also shown is a 3D graphic of the tent.

(a) Draw the elevation and plan as shown.

(b) Project an end view in the direction of the arrow **P**.

(c) Draw the development of the conical surface **A**.

(d) Draw the development of the cylindrical surface **B**.

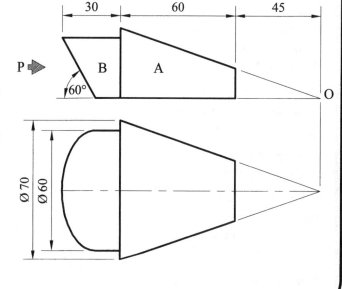

5 The figure shows a logo for dog kennels.
The figure is subject to transformations in the following order:

- Axial symmetry
- Central symmetry
- Translation
- Rotation clockwise through 90°.

P1, **P2**, **P3** and **P4** show the positions of point **P** under these transformations.

(a) Draw the given figure.

(b) Determine the image of the figure under **each** of these transformations.

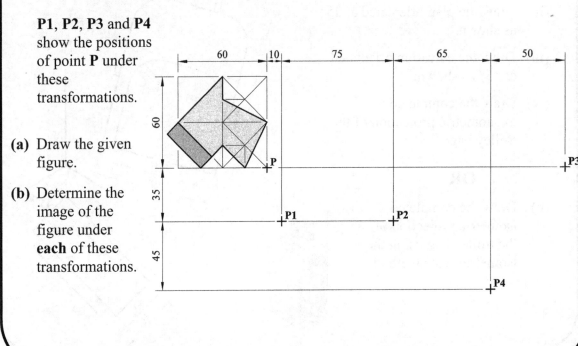

6 The figure shows the design of a logo for a bird sanctuary.

The curve **ABC** is a parabola with vertex at **B**. The curve **DEG** is a semi-ellipse and point **P** is a point on the curve. Determine the length of the minor axis and draw the semi-ellipse **DEG**.

The curve **RS**, with its vertex at **R**, is identical to a portion of the parabola **ABC**.

Draw the curve **RS** showing clearly how to determine point **S**.

The line **AT** is a tangent to the circle from **A**.

Complete the given logo showing clearly all construction lines and points of contact.

Note: Choose your own dimensions for the eye of the bird.

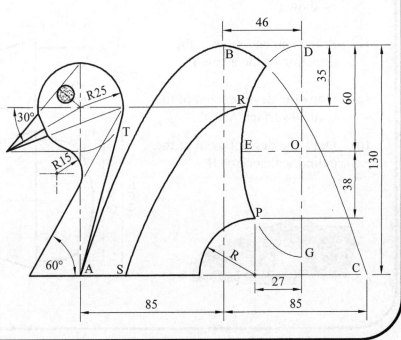

90

Coimisiún na Scrúduithe Stáit
State Examinations Commission

Junior Certificate Examination, 2010

Technical Graphics
Higher Level
Section A
(120 marks)

Monday, 21 June
Morning 9:30 - 12:30

Centre Number

Instructions

(a) Answer **any ten** questions in the spaces provided. All questions carry equal marks.

(b) Construction lines must be clearly shown.

(c) All measurements are in millimetres.

(d) This booklet must be handed up at the end of the examination.

(e) Write your examination number in the box provided below and on all other pages used.

Question	Mark
Section A	
1	
2	
3	
4	
5	
6	
TOTAL	
GRADE	

Examination Number: [   ]

SECTION A. Answer **any ten** questions. All questions carry equal marks.

1 Fill in the label for **each** item by selecting from the list on the right.

- Collinear
- Intersecting
- Parallel
- Perpendicular

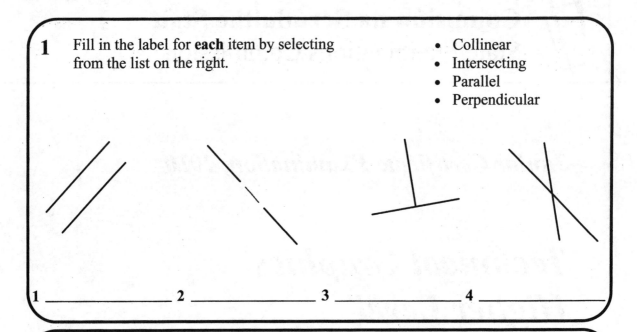

1 _____ 2 _____ 3 _____ 4 _____

2 The figure shows the incomplete perspective drawing of the outline of a house. A 3D graphic of the house is also shown. Complete the perspective drawing.

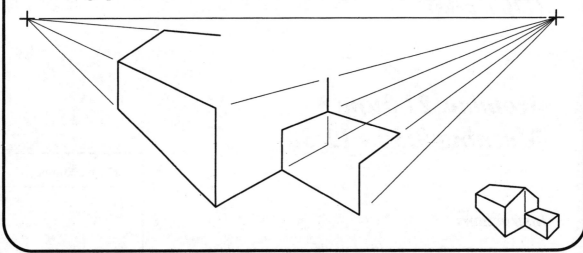

3 The figure shows the plan, elevation and a 3D graphic of a dust pan. Draw the development of the sides of the dust pan.
Note: It is not necessary to include the handle nor the back surface.

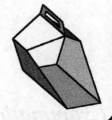

4 The elevation and end view of a writing desk are shown on the square grid.
Complete the pictorial sketch of the desk. Colour **or** shade the completed sketch.

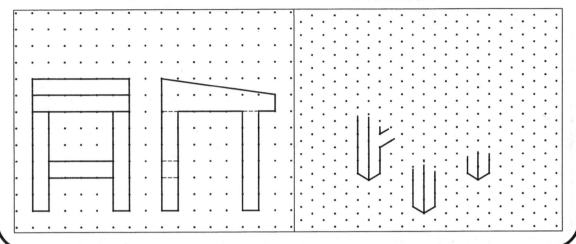

5 The figure shows the logo for a jewellery shop.
Draw a new logo similar to the given logo with length **AB** increased to **AB₁**.

Colour **or** shade the new logo.

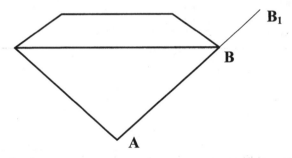

6 The **X** and **Y** axes shown are marked at intervals of 5 units.

Write down the coordinates of the vertices of the triangle **ABC**.

A _____

B _____

C _____

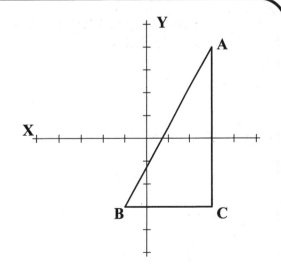

7 The figure shows the design for a handle of a knife.

The centres of the arcs are shown.

Show clearly all points of contact.

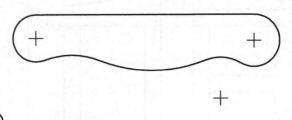

8 The plan and elevation of a desk lamp are shown.

In the space provided draw a **freehand pictorial sketch** of the desk lamp.

Colour **or** shade the sketch.

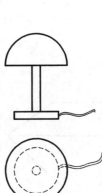

9 Write down **any three** CAD commands used to edit the figure shown in the sequence below.

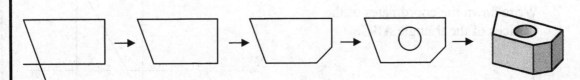

Any **three** CAD Commands: _____

_____

_____

10 The figure shows the outline plan and elevation of a crane and a load **ABC**.

A 3D graphic of the crane and load is also shown.

Complete the elevation of the crane and the load in the rotated position as shown by the broken line in plan.

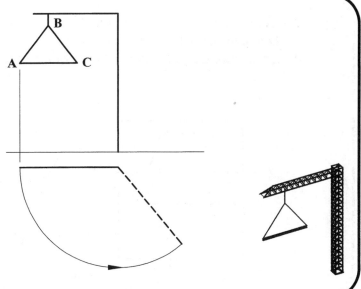

11 Write down the measure of the angles marked **A** and **B**.

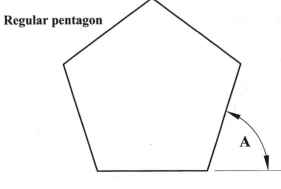

Regular pentagon

A = _____

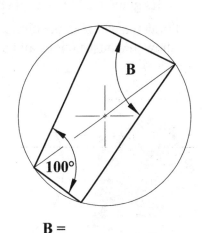

B = _____

12 Complete the plan of the truncated pyramid shown.

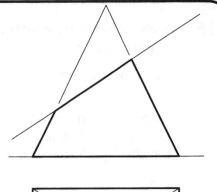

13 The figure shows the plan and elevation of a bridge.
A 3D graphic of the bridge is also shown.
Project an auxiliary elevation of the bridge on the **X₁Y₁** line shown.

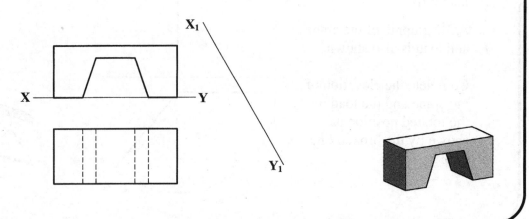

14 The figure shows the elevation of a bicycle rack and the wheel of a bicycle.
A 3D graphic of the wheel and rack is also shown.

Draw the wheel in position on the bicycle rack.
Show all constructions and points of contact.

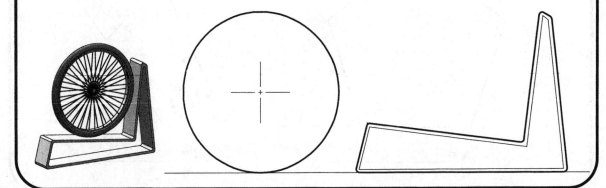

15 Twelve students were surveyed about their favourite sports.

The following were the results of the survey:

Football   - 6 students
Hurling   - 4 students
Basketball - 2 students.

Divide the given circle to represent
this information graphically as a pie chart.

Colour **or** shade the completed pie chart.

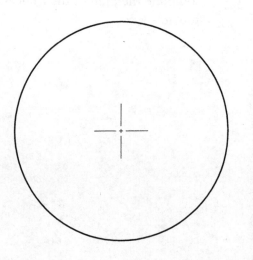

2010. S61B

Coimisiún na Scrúduithe Stáit
State Examinations Commission

Junior Certificate Examination, 2010

Technical Graphics
Higher Level
Section B
(280 marks)

Monday, 21 June
Morning 9:30 - 12:30

Instructions

(a)   Answer **any four** questions.

(b)   All questions in this section carry equal marks.

(c)   The number of the question must be distinctly marked by the side of each answer.

(d)   Work on **one side** of the answer paper only.

(e)   Write your examination number on each sheet of paper used.

SECTION B. Answer **any four** questions. All questions carry equal marks.

1 A pictorial view of a model of a castle is shown.

(a) Draw an elevation in the direction of arrow **A**.

(b) Project a plan from the elevation.

(c) Project an end view in the direction of arrow **B**.

(d) Determine the true shape of surface **S**.

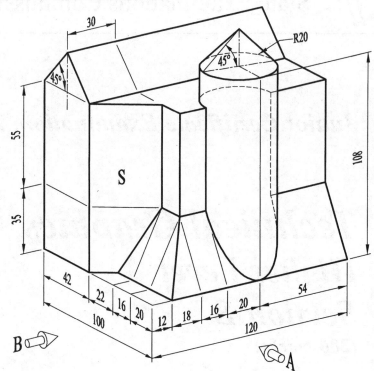

2 The figure shows the elevation and end view of a flap for a waste paper bin. The flap is transparent and shows a recycling logo. A 3D graphic of the bin is also shown. The flap is rotated about point **O**, as shown by the broken line in the end view.

(a) Draw the given elevation and end view.

(b) Project an elevation of the flap in the direction of arrow **A** to show the flap and logo in the rotated position.

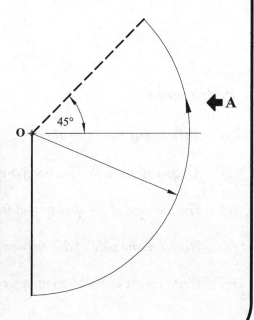

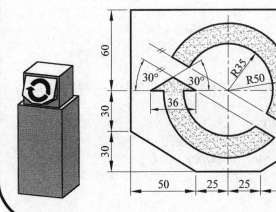

3 The axonometric axes required for the isometric projection of a rainwater storage tank are shown.

The plan and end elevation of the storage tank are shown in their required positions.

A 3D graphic of the storage tank is also shown.

(a)
(i) Draw the axonometric axes as shown.

(ii) Draw the plan orientated at 45° as shown.

(iii) Draw the end elevation orientated at 15° as shown.

(iv) Draw the completed axonometric projection of the storage tank.

OR

(b) Draw the completed isometric projection of the storage tank using the isometric scale method.

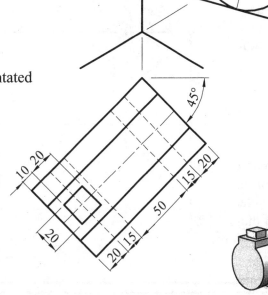

4 The figure shows the elevation and end view of a design for a covered stand for a sports stadium. A 3D graphic of the stand is also shown.

(a) Draw the given elevation and end view of the stand.

(b) Project a plan from the elevation.

(c) Draw the development of the curved surface **A**.

(d) Draw the development of the sloping surface **B**.

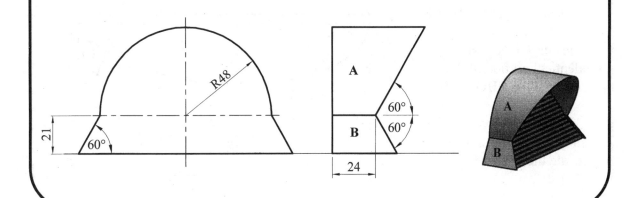

2010 HL

5 The figure shows the logo for a butterfly farm.
The figure is subject to transformations in the following order:

- Axial Symmetry
- Translation
- Central Symmetry
- Rotation anti-clockwise through 120°.

P1, **P2**, **P3** and **P4** show the positions of point **P** under each of these transformations.

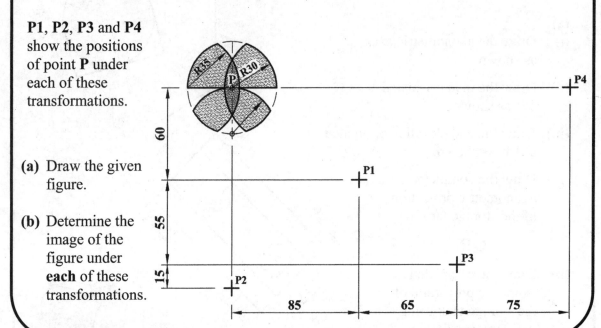

(a) Draw the given figure.

(b) Determine the image of the figure under **each** of these transformations.

---

6 The figure shows the design of a logo for a sailing club.

The curve **AB** is a parabola with the vertex at **A**.

The curve **CDG** is a semi-ellipse with focal points at **F₁** and **F₂**.
Determine the major and minor axes and draw the semi-ellipse **CDG**.

The line **EH** is a tangent to the semi-ellipse **CDG** at **E**.

The curve **LM** is an identical portion of the semi-ellipse **CDG**.

Complete the given design showing clearly how to locate the point **M**.

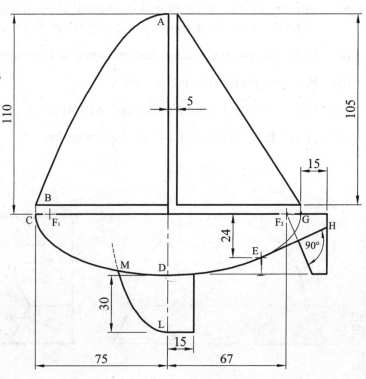

Coimisiún na Scrúduithe Stáit
State Examinations Commission

Junior Certificate Examination, 2019

Technical Graphics
Ordinary Level
Section A
(120 marks)

Monday, 17 June
Morning 9:30 - 12:00

Centre Number

Instructions

(a) Answer **any ten** questions in the spaces provided. All questions carry equal marks.

(b) Construction lines must be clearly shown.

(c) All measurements are in millimetres.

(d) This booklet must be handed up at the end of the examination.

(e) Write your examination number in the box provided below and on all other pages used.

Examination Number:

Question	Mark
Section A	
1	
2	
3	
4	
5	
6	
TOTAL	
GRADE	

SECTION A. Answer **any ten** questions. All questions carry equal marks.

1. Shown is an **incomplete** elevation and end view of a block weight. Also shown is a 3D graphic of the block weight.

Insert the missing lines in the elevation.

2. In the space provided, make a **freehand pictorial sketch** of the rugby tackle bag shown below.

Colour **or** shade the completed sketch.

3. List **one** advantage and **one** disadvantage of using a laptop computer.

Advantage:

_____

_____

Disadvantage:

_____

_____

4. **Fig. 1** shows a logo for a make-up counter inscribed in the square **ABCD**.

Complete the enlarged logo in the given square **ABCD** in **Fig. 2**.

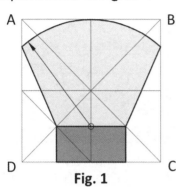

Fig. 1

A   B

D   C

Fig. 2

5. **Fig. 1** shows the outline of a comb, based on an ellipse.

The line **PT** is a tangent to the ellipse at **P**. Locate the focal points in **Fig. 2** and complete the comb by drawing the tangent **PT**.

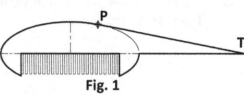

Fig. 1

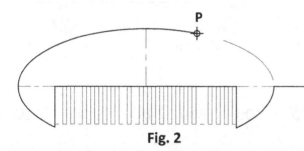

Fig. 2

6. The elevation and plan of a door wedge are shown.

Make a well-proportioned **freehand sketch** of the wedge in the space provided.

Colour **or** shade the completed sketch.

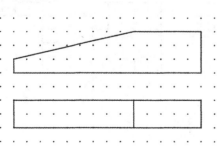

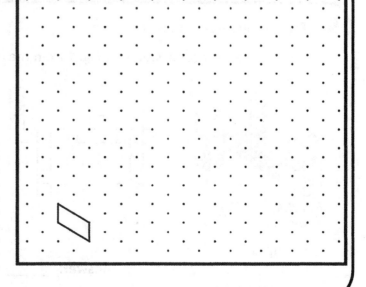

7. The outline of a hall mirror is shown.
Also shown is a 3D graphic of the mirror.

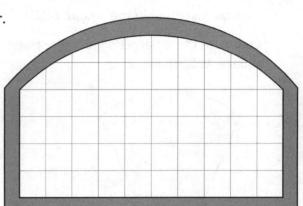

Write down the area of the glass in square units.

1 square = 1 square unit.

Area of the glass = _____ square units.

8. Using the scale provided, **measure** and **write down** the dimensions **A** and **B** of the skateboard shown.

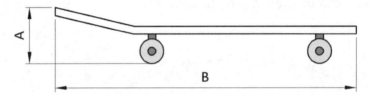

A: _____

B: _____

| 0 | 200 | 400 | 600 | 800 | 1000 | 1200 mm |

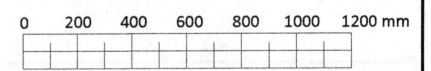

9. **Fig. 1** shows a set of blocks.

Choose the correct elevation for **Fig. 1** from the options shown in **Fig. 2** below.

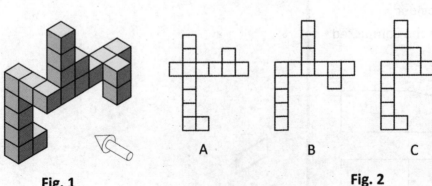

A   B   C   D

Fig. 1   **Fig. 2**

Answer:_____

10. The figure on the right shows the incomplete outline of a hook.
Also shown is a 3D graphic of the hook.

Complete the drawing of the hook by constructing a tangent from the centre-point **P** to the circle **C**.

Show all construction and the point of contact for this tangent.

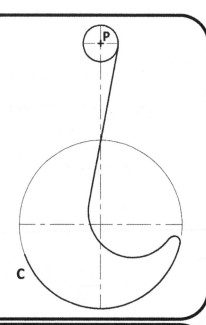

11. Write down **any two** CAD commands used to create the drawing of the plug.

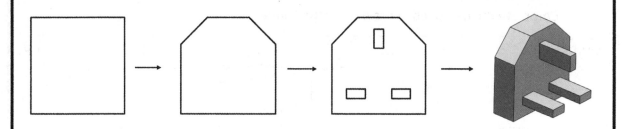

Any **two** CAD commands: _____

_____

12. The figure shows an incomplete block wall construction.

Write down the number of blocks required to complete the wall, as shown by the broken lines.

It will require _____ blocks to complete the wall construction.

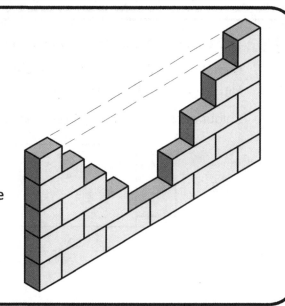

13. **Fig. 1** shows the design for a glamping logo.
The design is constructed using **50°** and **65°** angles.

Fig. 2 shows an **incomplete** drawing
of the logo. Complete the logo by
drawing a line at **50°** at point
A and at **65°** at point **B**.

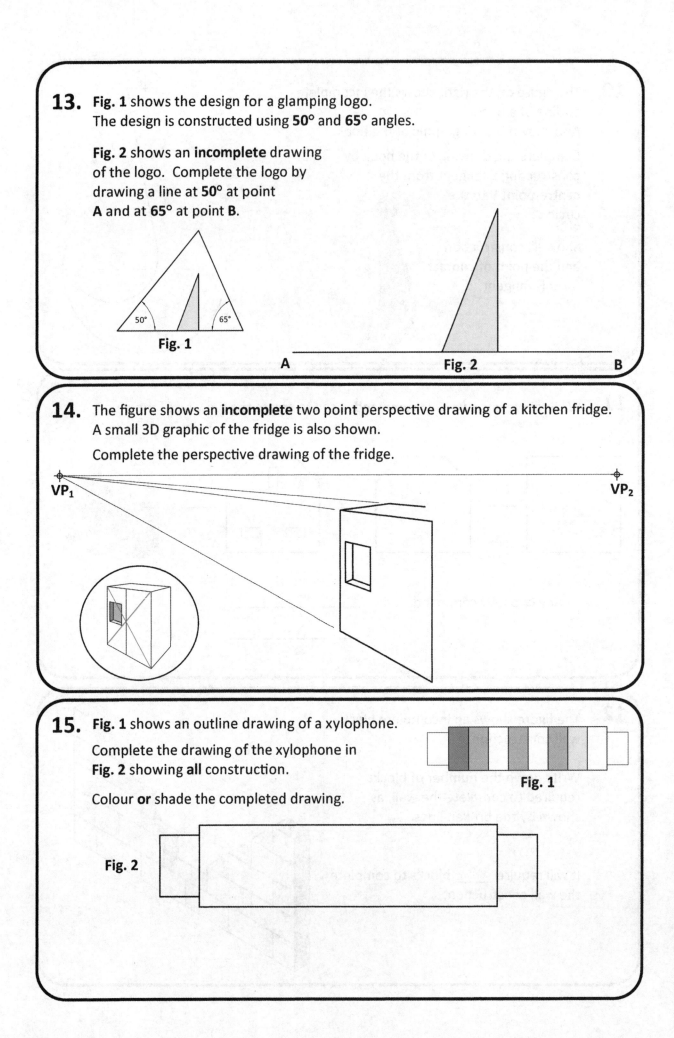

50° 65°

Fig. 1

A   **Fig. 2**   B

14. The figure shows an **incomplete** two point perspective drawing of a kitchen fridge.
A small 3D graphic of the fridge is also shown.

Complete the perspective drawing of the fridge.

VP₁   VP₂

15. **Fig. 1** shows an outline drawing of a xylophone.

Complete the drawing of the xylophone in
Fig. 2 showing **all** construction.

Colour **or** shade the completed drawing.

Fig. 1

Fig. 2

Coimisiún na Scrúduithe Stáit
State Examinations Commission

Junior Certificate Examination, 2019

Technical Graphics
Ordinary Level
Section B

(280 marks)

Monday, 17 June
Morning 9:30 - 12:00

Instructions

(a) Answer **any four** questions. All questions carry equal marks.

(b) The number of the question must be distinctly written by the side of each answer.

(c) Work on **one side** of the answer paper only.

(d) Write your examination number on each sheet of paper used.

SECTION B. Answer **any four** questions. All questions carry equal marks.

1. The figure shows a design for a cordless phone.
A 3D graphic of the phone is also shown.

Draw:

(a) An elevation in the direction of arrow **A**.

(b) An end view in the direction of arrow **B**.

(c) Insert **any four** dimensions.

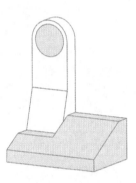

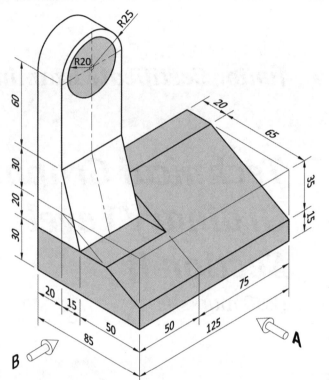

2. The graphic shows an outline design for a ***Darth Vader*** helmet.
The design is based on an ellipse and circles as shown.

The curve **ABC** is a semi-ellipse.

BO is half the **major axis** of the ellipse and is 80 mm long.

AO is half the **minor axis** and is 60 mm long.

Draw the given semi-ellipse and complete the design showing all constructions.

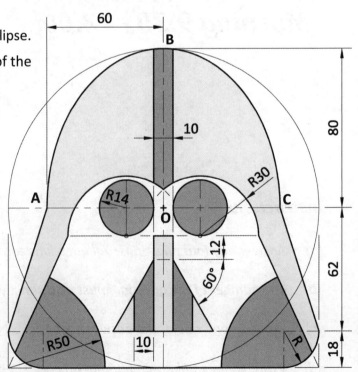

3. The graphics show a child's ball pond.

Draw:

(a) An elevation in the direction of arrow **A**.

(b) A plan projected from the elevation.

(c) The complete **surface development** of the ball pond.

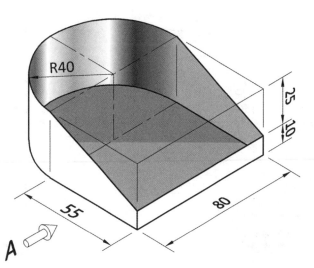

R40

55

80

25

10

A

4.

240

105

10

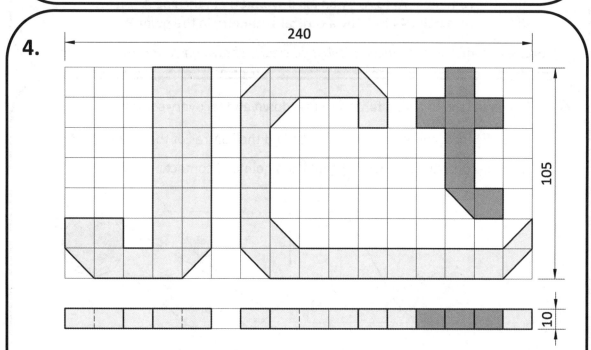

The figure shows the elevation and plan of the Junior Cycle for Teachers (**JCT**) logo.

The grid in elevation is made up of 15 mm squares and the thickness in plan is 10 mm.

Draw **one** of the following views: **(a)** An **isometric** view of the logo.

or

(b) An **oblique** view of the logo.

Note: *The solution must be presented on standard drawing paper.*

5. The graphics show the design of a blue flag logo displayed at some beaches.

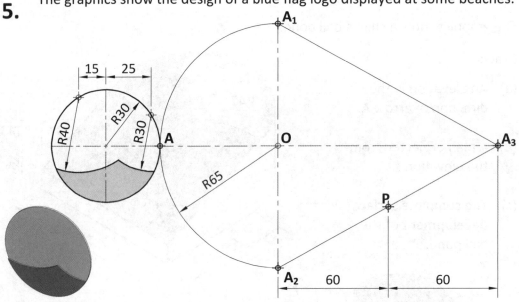

(a) Draw the given logo and then locate the points **A, A₁, A₂, A₃, O** and **P** as shown.

(b) Find the image of the given logo under the following transformations:

  (i) From point A to A₁ by a **translation**
  (ii) From point A₁ to A₂ by an **axial symmetry** in the line **A - A₃**
  (iii) From point A₂ to A₃ by a **central symmetry** in the point **P**.

Note: *All geometric constructions must be clearly shown on your drawing sheet.*

6. The figure shows a logo for a car breakdown and recovery company.

Draw the logo, showing clearly how to find the centres of the circles shown.

Show all construction lines, tangents and points of contact.

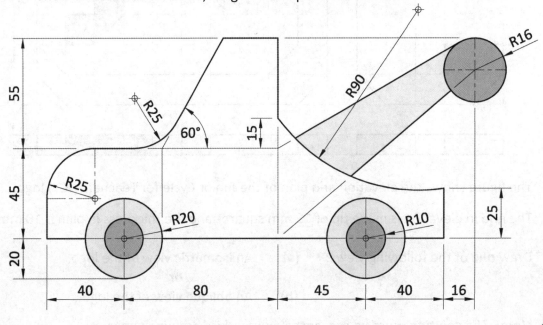

110

Coimisiún na Scrúduithe Stáit
State Examinations Commission

2018 OL

Junior Certificate Examination, 2018

Technical Graphics
Ordinary Level
Section A
(120 marks)

Monday, 18 June
Morning 9:30 - 12:00

Centre Number

Question	Mark
Section A	
1	
2	
3	
4	
5	
6	
TOTAL	
GRADE	

Instructions

(a) Answer **any ten** questions in the spaces provided.
      All questions carry equal marks.

(b) Construction lines must be clearly shown.

(c) All measurements are in millimetres.

(d) This booklet must be handed up at the end of the examination.

(e) Write your examination number in the box provided below
      and on all other pages used.

Examination Number:

SECTION A. Answer **any ten** questions. All questions carry equal marks.

---

1. Shown is the elevation and **incomplete** end view of a sewing machine. Also shown is a 3D graphic of the sewing machine.

Insert the missing lines in the end view.

---

2. In the space provided, make a **freehand pictorial sketch** of the flower-pot shown below.

Colour **or** shade the completed sketch.

---

3. Using a (✓) identify whether **each** of the following is an Input or Output device.

Input	Device	Output
	Mouse	
	Keyboard	
	Monitor	
	Speakers	
	Scanner	
	Printer	

4. **Fig. 1** shows a logo for a satellite TV company inscribed in the square **ABCD**.

Complete the enlarged logo in the given square **ABCD** in **Fig. 2**.

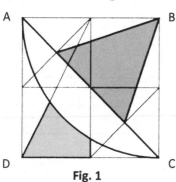

Fig. 1

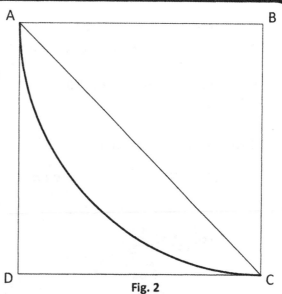

Fig. 2

---

5. **Fig. 1** shows the outline of a bridge based on an ellipse.

F_1 and F_2 are the focal points of the ellipse. Locate the focal points in **Fig. 2** and complete the outline of the bridge.

Fig. 1

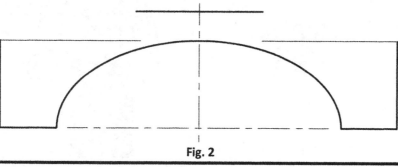

Fig. 2

---

6. The elevation and end view of an ATM (cash machine) are shown.

Make a well-proportioned **freehand sketch** of the ATM in the space provided.

Colour **or** shade the completed sketch.

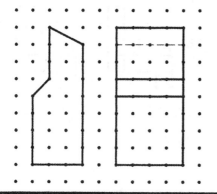

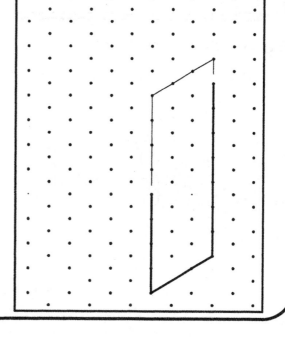

113

7. The outline of a floor tile design is shown.
Also shown is a 3D graphic of the floor tiles.

Write down the area of the tile in
square units.

1 square = 1 square unit.

Area of the tile = _____ square units.

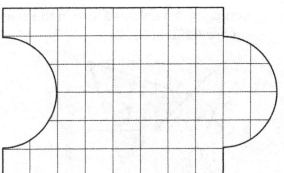

8. Using the scale provided, **measure** and
write down the dimensions **A** and **B** for
the *LEGO* man shown.

A: _____

B: _____

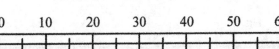

9. **Fig.1** shows a set of blocks.

Choose the correct elevation for **Fig.1** from the options shown in **Fig.2** below.

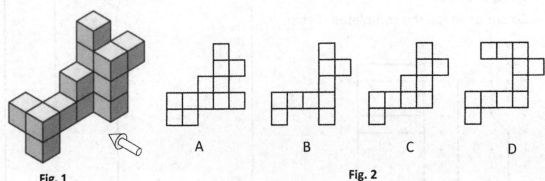

Fig. 1

A   B   C   D

Fig. 2

Answer:_____

10. The figure on the right shows the incomplete outline of a 'fidget spinner'. Also shown is a 3D graphic of the fidget spinner.

Complete the drawing of the fidget spinner.
Show all construction and **all** points of contact.

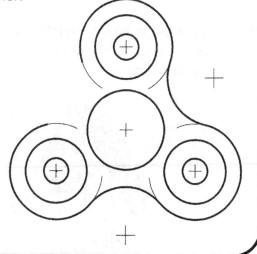

11. Write down **any two** CAD commands used to create the drawing of the music app logo.

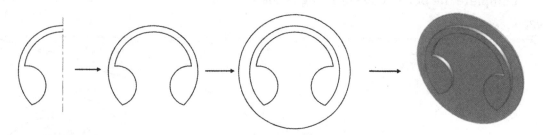

Any **two** CAD commands: _____

_____

12. Count the number of **squares** and **rectangles** in the diagram.

Squares: _____

Rectangles: _____

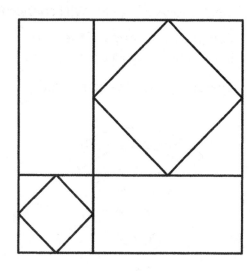

13. **Fig. 1** shows the design of a logo for a racing team. The design is based on a regular hexagon.

Fig. 2 shows an **incomplete** drawing of the logo. Complete the drawing showing all construction.

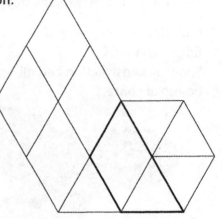

Fig. 1

Fig. 2

14. The figure shows an **incomplete** two point perspective drawing of a soccer dug-out. A small 3D graphic of the dug-out is also shown.

Complete the perspective drawing of the dug-out.

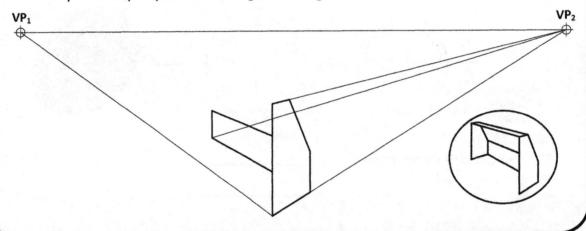

15. **Fig. 1** shows a logo for WiFi connection.

Complete the design of the logo in **Fig. 2** showing **all** construction.

Colour **or** shade the completed logo.

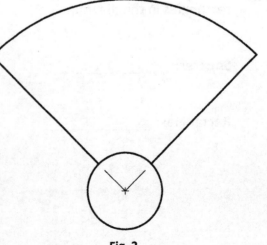

Fig. 1

Fig. 2

Coimisiún na Scrúduithe Stáit
State Examinations Commission

Junior Certificate Examination, 2018

Technical Graphics
Ordinary Level
Section B
(280 marks)

Monday, 18 June
Morning 9:30 - 12:00

Instructions

(a) Answer **any four** questions. All questions carry equal marks.

(b) The number of the question must be distinctly marked by the side of each answer.

(c) Work on **one side** of the answer paper only.

(d) Write your examination number on each sheet of paper used.

SECTION B. Answer **any four** questions. All questions carry equal marks.

1. The figure shows a design for a toy space shuttle.
   A 3D graphic is also shown.

   Draw:

   (a) An elevation in the direction of arrow **A**.

   (b) A plan projected from the elevation.

   (c) Insert **any four** dimensions.

   Note: *Some hidden detail has been included for clarity.*

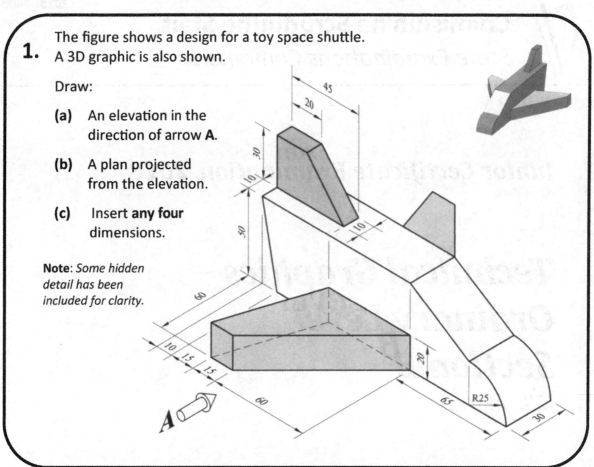

2. The graphic shows a design for an *Art Shop logo*.
   The design is based on an ellipse and circles as shown.

   The curve **ABCD** is an ellipse.
   AC is the **major axis** of the ellipse and is 150 mm long.
   OD is half the **minor axis** and is 50 mm long.

   Draw the given ellipse and complete the design showing all constructions.

   Note:
   *All **five** 'colour pot' circles are **R 10**.*

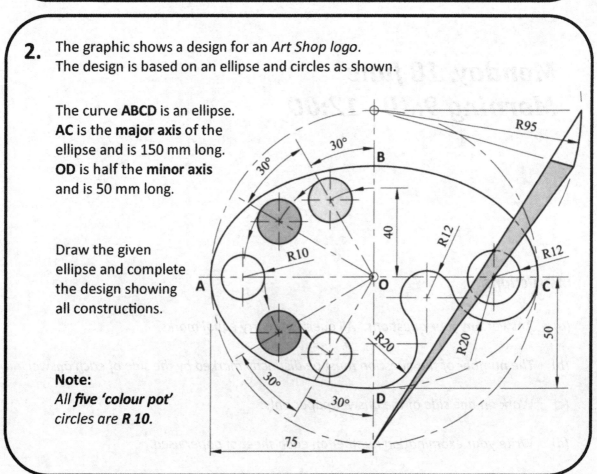

3. The graphics show a tape dispenser.

Draw:
(a) An elevation in the direction of arrow **A**.

(b) An end view in the direction of arrow **B**.

(c) The complete **surface development** of the tape dispenser.

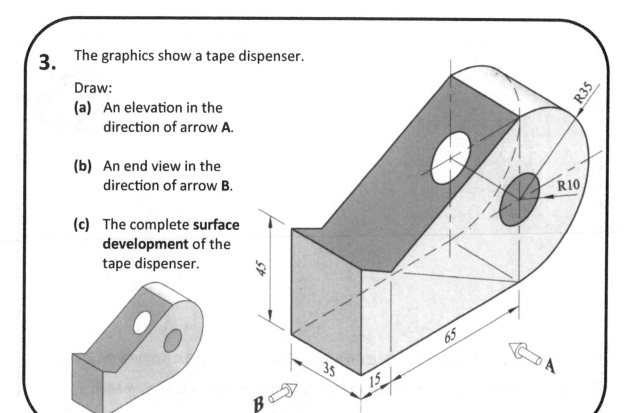

4.

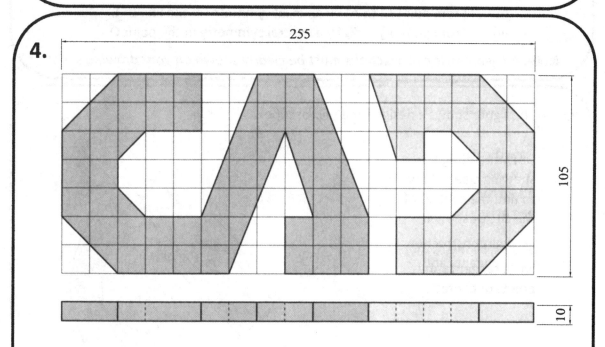

The figure shows the elevation and plan of a **CAD** (Computer Aided Design) logo.

The grid in elevation is made up of 15 mm squares and the thickness in plan is 10 mm.

Draw **one** of the following views: **(a)** An **isometric** view of the logo.

or

(b) An **oblique** view of the logo.

Note: The solution must be presented on standard drawing paper.

The graphics show the design of a logo for 'CloudKey' online data storage.

5.

60

60 60

10

A **L** **A₃**

50

O

50

30

A₁ **L₁** **A₂**

(a) Draw the given logo and then locate the points **A, A₁, A₂, A₃** and **O** as shown.

(b) Find the image of the given logo under the following transformations:

    (i) From point A to A₁ by a **translation**

    (ii) From point A₁ to A₂ by an **axial symmetry** in the line **L - L₁**

    (iii) From point A₂ to A₃ by a **central symmetry** in the point **O**.

Note: *All geometric constructions must be clearly shown on your drawing sheet.*

6. The figure shows a design for a microscope.

Draw the design
showing clearly how
to find the centres of
the circles shown.

Show all construction
lines, tangents and
points of contact.

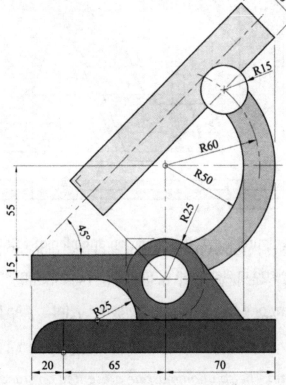

30

R15

R60

R50

R25

55

45°

15

R25

20 65 70

120

Coimisiún na Scrúduithe Stáit
State Examinations Commission

Junior Certificate Examination, 2017

Technical Graphics
Ordinary Level
Section A
(120 marks)

Monday, 19 June
Morning 9:30 - 12:00

Centre Number

Instructions

(a) Answer **any ten** questions in the spaces provided.
All questions carry equal marks.

(b) Construction lines must be clearly shown.

(c) All measurements are in millimetres.

(d) This booklet must be handed up at the end of the examination.

(e) Write your examination number in the box provided below
and on all other pages used.

Examination Number:

Question	Mark
Section A	
1	
2	
3	
4	
5	
6	
TOTAL	
GRADE	

SECTION A. Answer **any ten** questions. All questions carry equal marks.

1. Shown is the elevation and **incomplete** end view of a computer printer. Also shown is a 3D graphic of the printer.

Insert the missing lines in the end view.

2. In the space provided, make a **freehand pictorial sketch** of the sports cone shown below.

Colour **or** shade the completed sketch.

3. Name the computer related items **A** and **B** shown below.

A_____   B_____

Give **one** advantage of item **A** over item **B**.

_____

_____

4. **Fig. 1** shows a logo for a car clamping company inscribed in the square **ABCD**.

Draw the enlarged logo in the given square **ABCD** in **Fig. 2**.

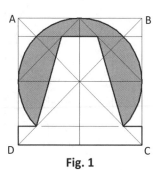

Fig. 1

A   B

D   C

Fig. 2

---

5. **Fig. 1** shows the outline of a chef's hat based on an ellipse and a rectangle.

F_1 and F_2 are the focal points of the ellipse. Locate the focal points in **Fig. 2** and complete the outline by drawing the rectangle **ABCD** as shown.

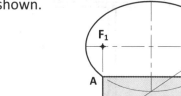

Fig. 1

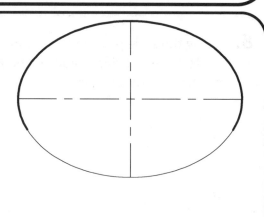

Fig. 2

---

6. The elevation and end view of an electric car charging point are shown.

Make a well proportioned **freehand sketch** of the charging point in the space provided.

Colour **or** shade the completed sketch.

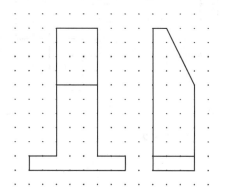

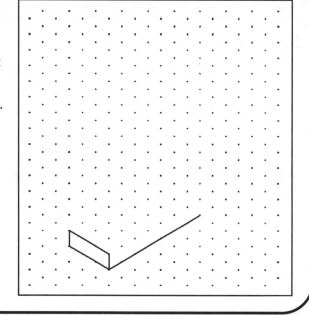

123

7. The outline of a label for a bottle is shown.
Also shown is a 3D graphic of the label on the bottle.

Write down the area of the label in square units.

1 square = 1 square unit.

Area of the label = _____ square units.

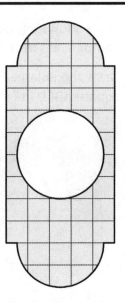

---

8. Using the scale provided, **measure** and **write down** the dimensions **A** and **B** for the basketball stand shown.

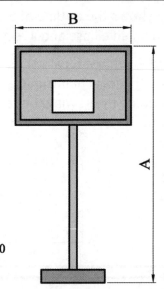

A: _____

B: _____

0   20   40   60   80   100 120 140 160 180 200

---

9. **Fig.1** shows a set of blocks.

Choose the correct elevation for **Fig.1** from the options shown in **Fig.2** below.

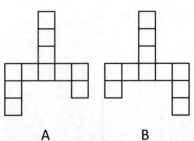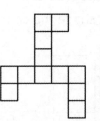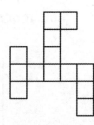

A   B   C   D

Fig. 1   **Fig. 2**

Answer:_____

10. The figure shows the incomplete outline of a golf club. Also shown is a 3D graphic of the club.

Complete the drawing of the golf club by constructing a tangent from point **P** to the circle **C**.

Show all construction and the point of contact.

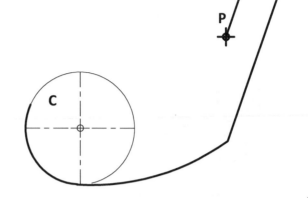

11. Write down **any two** CAD commands used to create the drawing of the try-square.

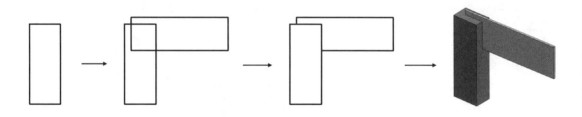

Any **two** CAD commands: _____

_____

12. Twelve students were surveyed about the type of music that they listened to.

Shade the pie chart to represent the following results from the survey.

- Pop - **6** students
- Rock - **4** students
- R & B - **2** students

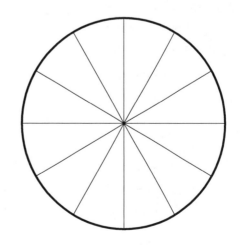

13. **Fig. 1** shows a design for a windfarm logo. The design is based on a regular hexagon and arcs as shown.

Fig. 2 shows an **incomplete** drawing of the design. Complete the drawing showing all constructions.

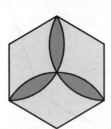

Fig. 1

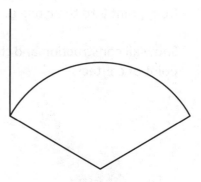

Fig. 2

14. The figure shows an **incomplete** two point perspective drawing of a table-tennis table. A 3D graphic of the table is also shown.

Complete the perspective drawing of the table.

VP₁

VP₂

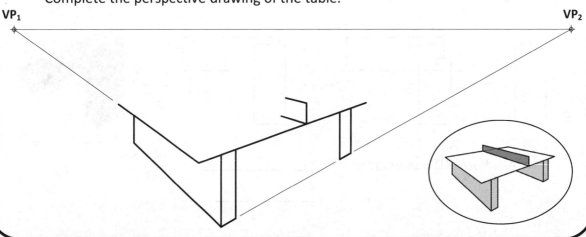

15. **Fig. 1** shows a logo for a badminton club.

Complete the design of the logo in **Fig. 2** by constructing an axial symmetry in the line **LL₁**.

Colour **or** shade the completed logo.

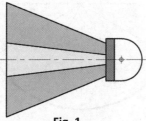

Fig. 1

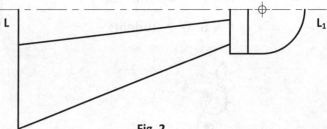

Fig. 2

Coimisiún na Scrúduithe Stáit
State Examinations Commission

Junior Certificate Examination, 2017

Technical Graphics
Ordinary Level
Section B
(280 marks)

Monday, 19 June
Morning 9:30 - 12:00

Instructions

(a)   Answer **any four** questions. All questions carry equal marks.

(b)   The number of the question must be distinctly marked by the side of each answer.

(c)   Work on **one side** of the answer paper only.

(d)   Write your examination number on each sheet of paper used.

SECTION B. Answer **any four** questions. All questions carry equal marks.

1. The figure shows a design for a toy tug boat.
A 3D graphic is also shown.

Draw:

(a) An elevation in the direction of arrow **A**.

(b) A plan projected from the elevation.

(c) Insert **any four** dimensions.

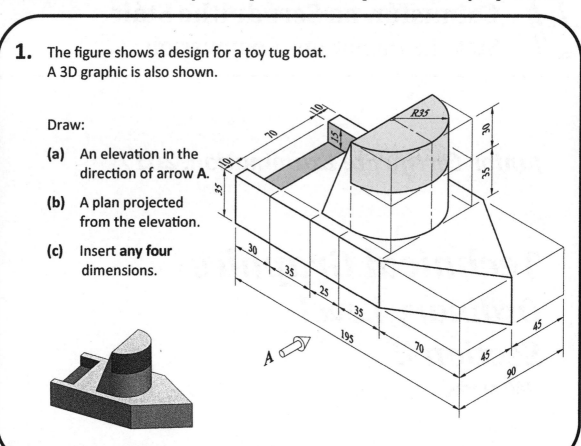

2. The graphic shows a design for an *angry bird* character.
The design is based on circles and an ellipse as shown.

The curve **ABCD** is an ellipse. **AC** is the **major axis** of the ellipse and is 160 mm long. **OD** is half the **minor axis** and is 60 mm long.

Draw the given ellipse and complete the design showing clearly all constructions.

Note: *Choose your own dimension for the pupils of the eyes.*

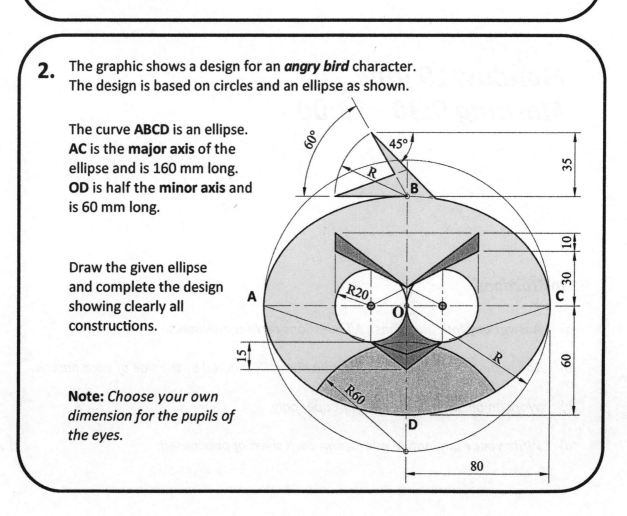

3. The graphics show a bicycle shelter.

Draw:
(a) An elevation in the direction of arrow **A**.

(b) An end view in the direction of arrow **B**.

(c) The complete **surface development** of the bicycle shelter.

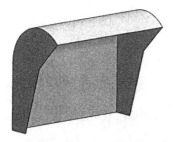

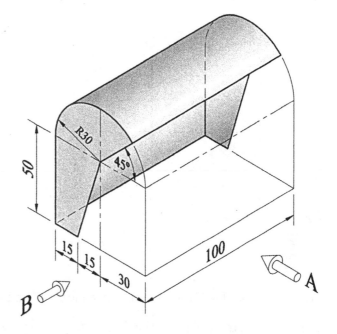

4.

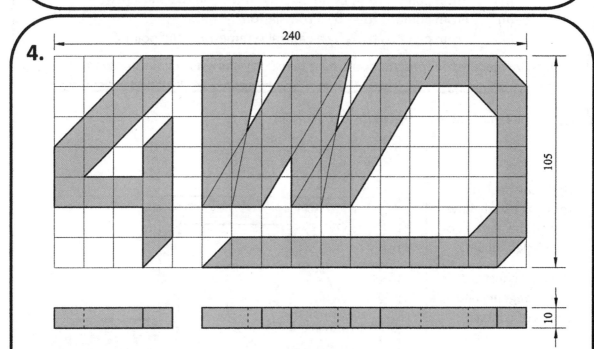

The figure shows the elevation and plan of a **4 W**heel **D**rive logo.

The grid in elevation is made up of 15 mm squares and the thickness in plan is 10 mm.

Draw **one** of the following views: **(a)** An **isometric** view of the logo.
or
(b) An **oblique** view of the logo.

Note: The solution must be presented on standard drawing paper.

129

5. The graphics show the design of a logo for a flower shop.

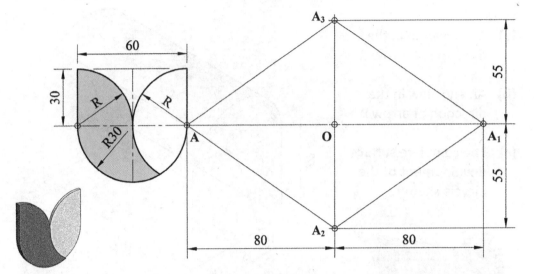

(a) Draw the given logo and then locate the points **A**, **A₁**, **A₂**, **A₃** and **O** as shown.

(b) Find the image of the given logo under the following transformations:

(i) From point A to A_1 by an **axial symmetry** in the line A_2-A_3
(ii) From point A_1 to A_2 by a **translation**
(iii) From point A_2 to A_3 by a **central symmetry** in the point **O**.

Note: *All geometric constructions must be clearly shown on your drawing.*

6. The figure shows a design for a toy forklift.

Draw the design showing clearly how to find the centres of the circles shown.

Show all construction lines, tangents and points of contact.

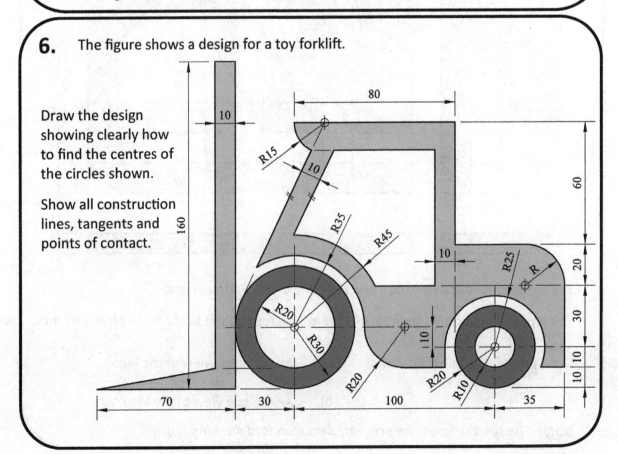

Coimisiún na Scrúduithe Stáit
State Examinations Commission

Junior Certificate Examination, 2016

Technical Graphics
Ordinary Level
Section A
(120 marks)

Monday, 20 June
Morning 9:30 - 12:00

Centre Number

Instructions

*(a)   Answer **any ten** questions in the spaces provided.
      All questions carry equal marks.*

(b)   Construction lines must be clearly shown.

(c)   All measurements are in millimetres.

(d)   This booklet must be handed up at the end of the examination.

*(e)   Write your examination number in the box provided below
      and on all other pages used.*

Examination Number:

Question	Mark
Section A	
1	
2	
3	
4	
5	
6	
TOTAL	
GRADE	

1. Shown is the **incomplete** elevation and end view of a lottery ticket scanner.

Also shown is a 3D graphic of the scanner.

Insert the missing lines in the elevation.

2. In the space provided, make a **freehand pictorial sketch** of the makeup bottle shown. Colour **or** shade the completed sketch.

3. Name the computer related item shown **and** state its use.

Name:

_____

Use:

_____

_____

132

4. **Fig. 1** shows a jewellery store logo inscribed in the square **ABCD**. Draw the enlarged logo in the given square **ABCD** in **Fig. 2**.

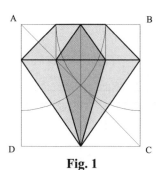

Fig. 1

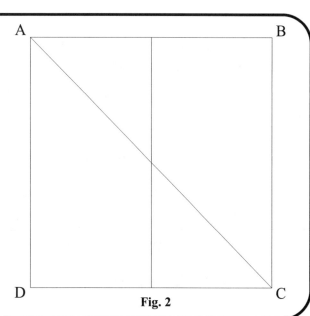

Fig. 2

5. **Fig. 1** shows a logo for a sailing company.

The line **PQ** is a tangent to the ellipse at **P**. Locate the focal points of the ellipse in **Fig. 2** and complete the sail by drawing the tangent **PQ**.

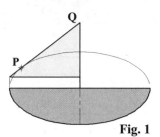

Fig. 1

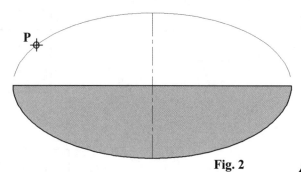

Fig. 2

6. The elevation and plan of a sun lounger are shown.

Make a well proportioned **freehand sketch** of the lounger in the space provided.

Colour **or** shade the completed sketch.

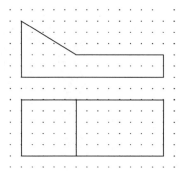

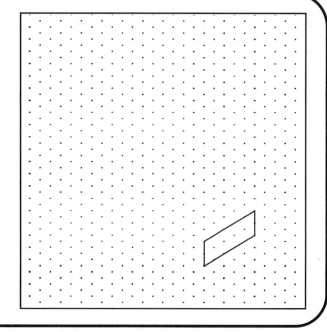

7. The outline of a jigsaw piece is shown.
Also shown is a 3D graphic of the jigsaw piece.

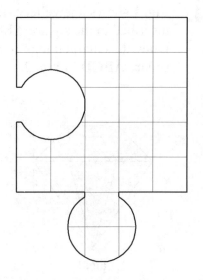

Write down the area of the jigsaw piece in square units.

1 square = 1 square unit.

Area of the jigsaw piece: _____ **square units**.

8. Using the scale provided, **measure** and **write down** the dimensions **A** and **B** for the couch shown.

A: _____

B: _____

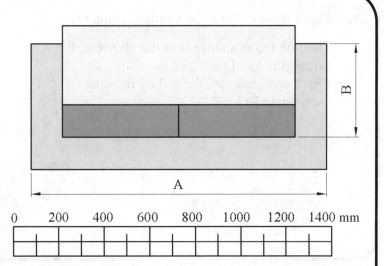

9. The figure shows a set of blocks.
Draw, in the space provided, an elevation of the blocks in the direction of the arrow.

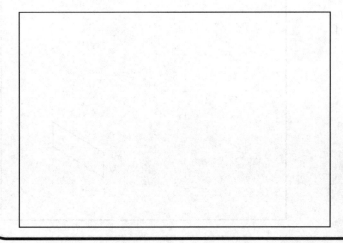

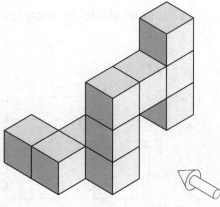

10. The figure shows the incomplete outline of a toy trumpet. Also shown is a 3D model of the trumpet.

Complete the drawing of the trumpet showing all constructions and points of contact.

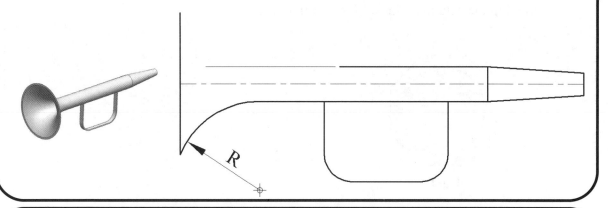

11. Write down **any two** CAD commands used to produce the drawing of the eraser.

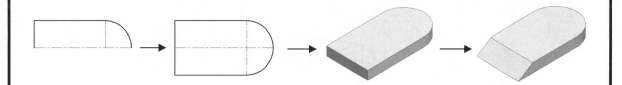

Any **two** CAD commands: _____

_____

12. Twenty four students were surveyed regarding their choice of lunch from the school canteen.

Shade the horizontal bar chart to indicate the following student choices.

Beef   - **4** students

Chicken - **8** students

Pasta   - **5** students

Salad   - **7** students

Beef

Chicken

Pasta

Salad

0   1   2   3   4   5   6   7   8   9

Number of Students

13. **Fig. 1** shows the plan of a trampoline.
The outline is based on a regular octagon.

Fig. 2 shows an **incomplete** plan view of a
similar trampoline. Complete the plan by
drawing the octagon. Show all constructions.

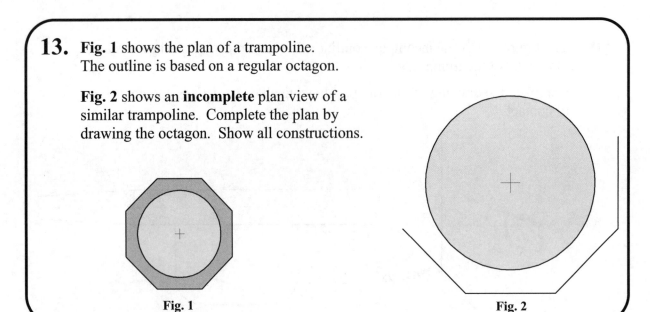

Fig. 1

Fig. 2

14. The figure shows an **incomplete** two-point perspective drawing of a stove.
A small 3D graphic of the stove is also shown.

Complete the perspective drawing of the stove.

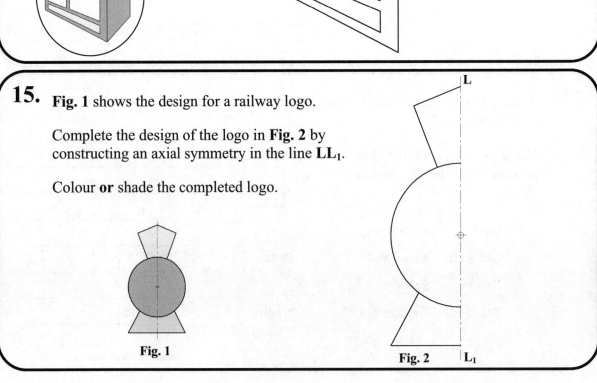

VP₁

VP₂

15. **Fig. 1** shows the design for a railway logo.

Complete the design of the logo in **Fig. 2** by
constructing an axial symmetry in the line **LL₁**.

Colour **or** shade the completed logo.

Fig. 1

Fig. 2

L

L₁

Coimisiún na Scrúduithe Stáit
State Examinations Commission

Junior Certificate Examination, 2016

Technical Graphics
Ordinary Level
Section B
(280 marks)

Monday, 20 June
Morning 9:30 - 12:00

2016 OL

Instructions

(a) Answer **any four** questions. All questions carry equal marks.

(b) The number of the question must be distinctly marked by the side of each answer.

(c) Work on **one side** of the answer paper only.

(d) Write your examination number on each sheet of paper used.

SECTION B. Answer **any four** questions. All questions carry equal marks.

1. The figure shows a design for a piano.
A 3D graphic is also shown.

Draw:

(a) An elevation in the direction of arrow **A**.

(b) An end view in the direction of arrow **B**.

(c) Insert **any four** dimensions.

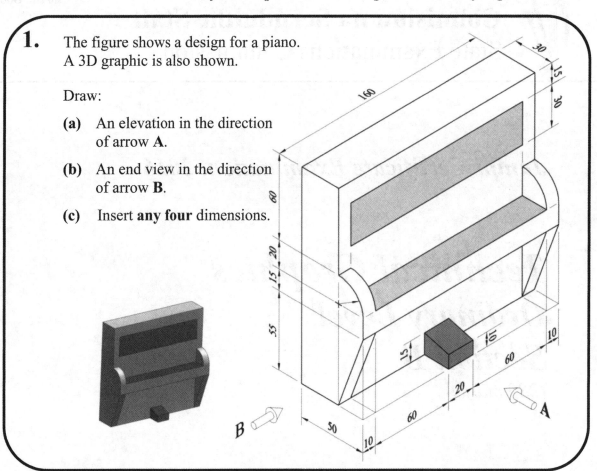

2. The graphics show the outline of a motorsport helmet.
The design is based on circles, parallel lines and a semi-ellipse as shown.

The curve **ABC** is a semi-ellipse. **AC** is the **major axis** of the ellipse and is 130 mm long. **OB** is half the **minor axis** and is 50 mm long.

Draw the given ellipse and complete the design showing clearly all constructions.

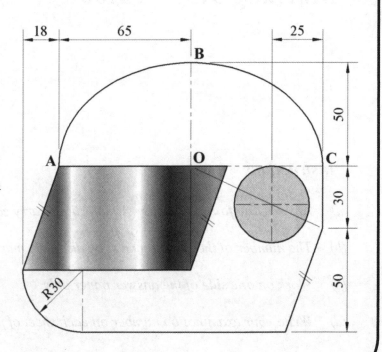

138

3. The figure shows the bucket of a toy mechanical digger.
A 3D graphic is also shown.

Draw:
(a) An elevation in the
direction of arrow **A**.

(b) A plan projected from
the elevation.

(c) The complete **surface
development** of the
bucket.

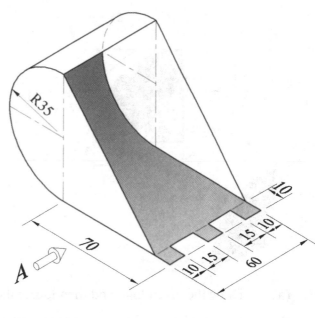

R35

70

A

10 15

15 10

60

10

4.

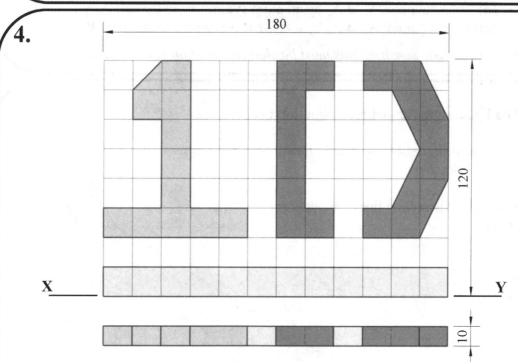

180

120

X

Y

10

The figure shows the elevation and plan of a band logo.

The grid in elevation is made up of 15 mm squares and the thickness in plan is 10 mm.

Draw **one** of the following views: **(a)** An **isometric** view of the initials.

or

(b) An **oblique** view of the initials.

Note: The solution must be presented on standard drawing paper.

139

5. The graphics show the design of a logo for a rugby tournament.

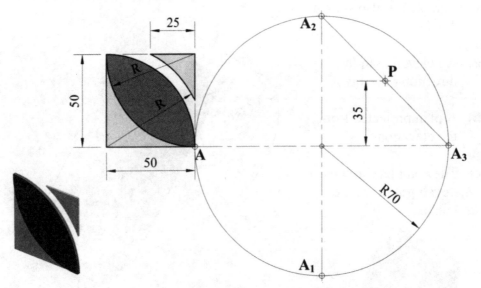

(a) Draw the given logo and then locate the points **A, A₁, A₂, A₃** and **P** as shown.

(b) Find the image of the given logo under the following transformations:

    (i)   From point A to A₁ by a **translation**;
    (ii)   From point A₁ to A₂ by an **axial symmetry** in the line **A-A₃**;
    (iii)   From point A₂ to A₃ by a **central symmetry** in the point **P**.

Note: *All geometric constructions must be clearly shown on your drawing sheet.*

---

6. The figure shows an outline design for a ladies shoe.

Draw the design showing clearly how to find the centres of the circles shown.

Show all construction lines, tangents and points of contact.

R32

60°

110

R25

R100

30   45   100   10

Coimisiún na Scrúduithe Stáit
State Examinations Commission

Junior Certificate Examination, 2015

Technical Graphics
Ordinary Level
Section A
(120 marks)

2015 OL

Monday, 15 June
Morning, 9:30 - 12:00

Centre Number

Instructions

(a) Answer **any ten** questions in the spaces provided. All questions carry equal marks.

(b) Construction lines must be clearly shown.

(c) All measurements are in millimetres.

(d) This booklet must be handed up at the end of the examination.

(e) Write your examination number in the box provided below and on all other pages used.

Examination Number:

Question	Mark
Section A	
1	
2	
3	
4	
5	
6	
TOTAL	
GRADE	

SECTION A. Answer **any ten** questions. All questions carry equal marks.

1. Shown is the elevation and **incomplete** end view of a walkie-talkie.

Also shown is a 3D graphic of the walkie-talkie.

Insert the missing lines in the end view.

2. In the space provided, make a **freehand pictorial sketch** of the spinning-top shown. Colour **or** shade the completed sketch.

3. Name the device shown and state its use.

Name: _____

Use: _____

_____

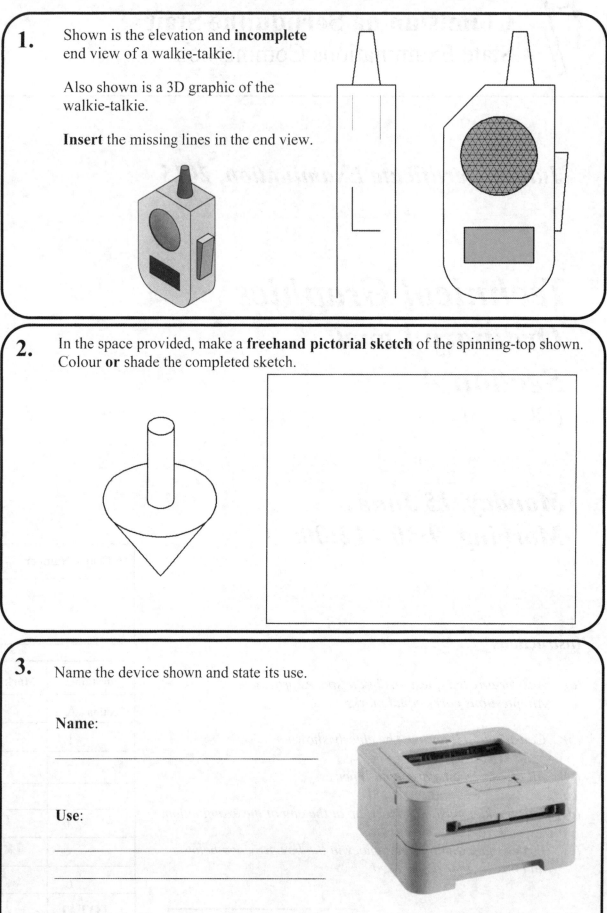

4. **Fig. 1** shows a school crest inscribed in the square **ABCD**.

Draw the enlarged crest in the given square **ABCD** in **Fig. 2**.

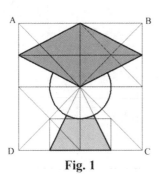

Fig. 1

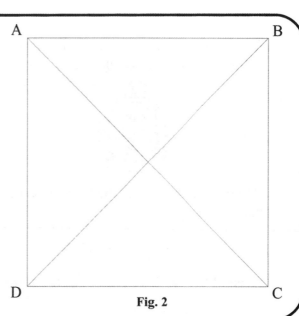

Fig. 2

5. **Fig. 1** shows the outline of a USB key based on an ellipse and a rectangle. F_1 and F_2 are the focal points of the ellipse. Locate the focal points in **Fig. 2** and complete the design by drawing the rectangle **ABCD** through F_2, as shown.

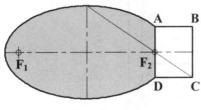

Fig. 1

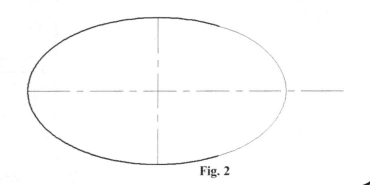

Fig. 2

6. The elevation and plan of a show-jumping wall are shown.

Make a well proportioned **freehand sketch** of the wall in the space provided.

Colour **or** shade the completed sketch.

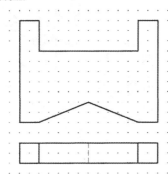

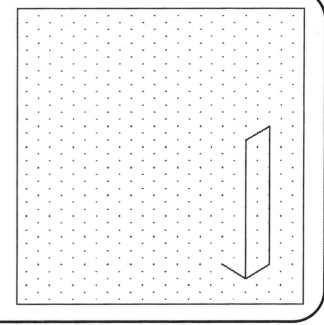

7. The outline of a birthday card is shown.
Also shown is a 3D graphic of the card.

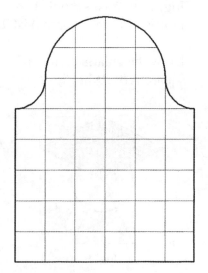

Write down the area of the birthday card in square units.

1 square = 1 square unit.

Area of the card: _____ **square units**.

8. Using the scale provided, **measure** and **write down** the dimensions **A** and **B** for the wood burning stove shown.

A: _____

B: _____

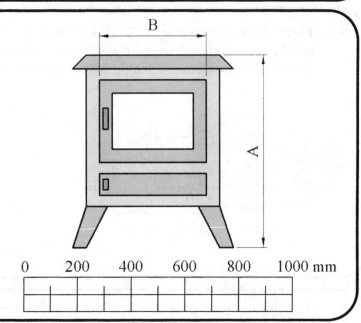

9. The figure shows a set of blocks.
Draw, in the space provided, an elevation of the blocks in the direction of the arrow.

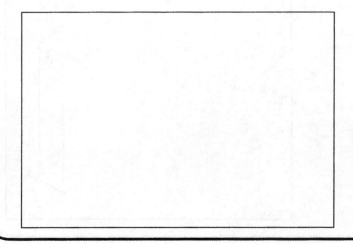

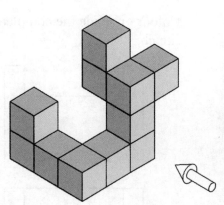

10. The figure shows the incomplete outline of a perfume bottle. Also shown is a 3D graphic of the bottle.

Complete the drawing of the bottle by constructing a tangent from point **P** to the circle **C**.

Show all construction and the point of contact.

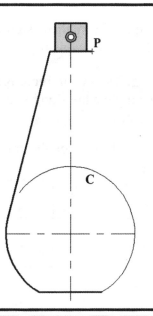

11. Write down **any two** CAD commands used to produce the drawing of the set-square.

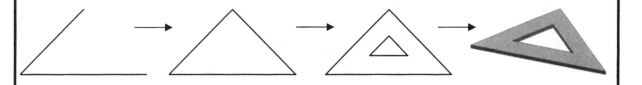

Any **two** CAD commands: _____

_____

12. A public address system has three speakers. The figure shows the volume control for each speaker.

Shade the volume controls to indicate the following speaker settings:

Speaker **1**: 70

Speaker **2**: 30

Speaker **3**: 50

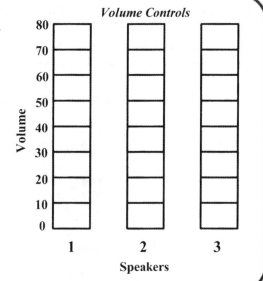

13. **Fig. 1** shows the design for a direction sign.
The sign is constructed using 25° angles.

Fig. 2 shows an **incomplete** view of the sign.
Complete the sign by drawing 25° angles at
point **P**.

Colour **or** shade the completed sign.

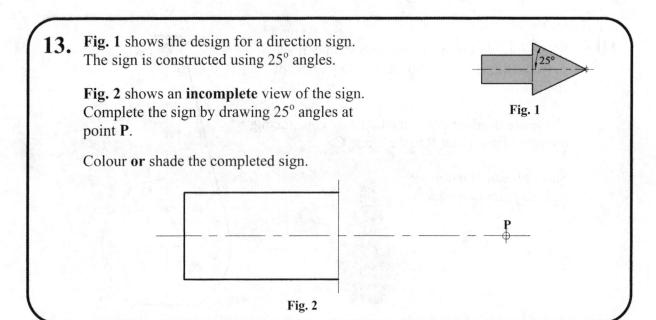

Fig. 1

Fig. 2

14. The figure shows an **incomplete** two point perspective drawing of a bed.
A small 3D graphic of the bed is also shown.
Complete the perspective drawing of the bed.

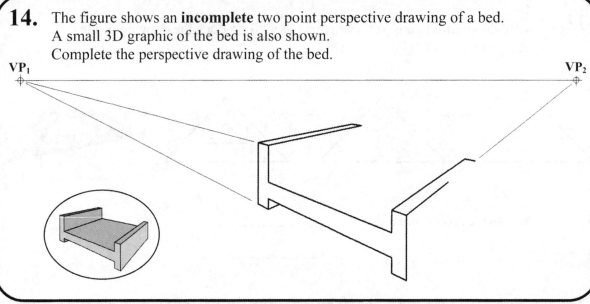

VP_1

VP_2

15. **Fig. 1** shows the design for a table lamp.

Complete the design of the lamp in **Fig. 2** by
constructing an axial symmetry in the line LL_1.

Colour **or** shade the completed lamp.

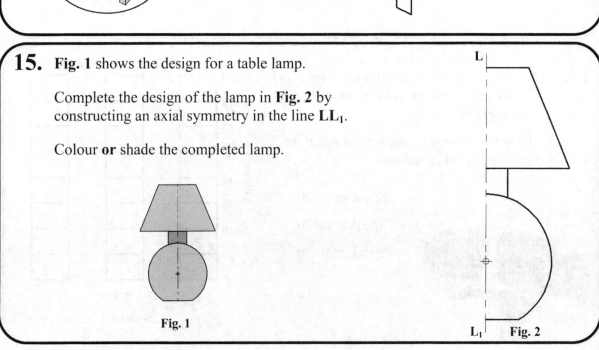

Fig. 1

L

L_1 **Fig. 2**

Coimisiún na Scrúduithe Stáit
State Examinations Commission

2015. S60B

Junior Certificate Examination, 2015

Technical Graphics
Ordinary Level
Section B
(280 marks)

Monday, 15 June
Morning, 9:30 - 12:00

Instructions

(a)   Answer **any four** questions. All questions carry equal marks.

(b)   The number of the question must be distinctly marked by the side of each answer.

(c)   Work on **one side** of the answer paper only.

(d)   Write your examination number on each sheet of paper used.

SECTION B. Answer **any four** questions. All questions carry equal marks.

1. The figure shows a design for a kitchen knife block.
A 3D graphic is also shown.

Draw:

(a) An elevation in the direction of arrow **A**.

(b) A plan projected from the elevation.

(c) Insert **any four** dimensions.

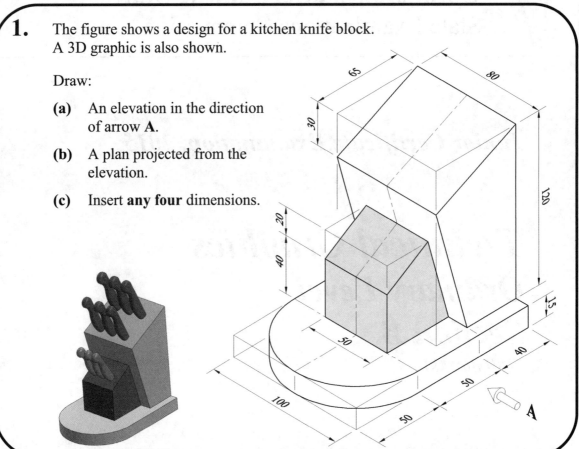

2. The graphics show the logo for a social media company (Hootsuite™).
The owl logo is based on circles and on an ellipse as shown.

The curve **ABCD** is an ellipse. **AC** is the **major axis** of the ellipse and is 120 mm long. **OD** is half the **minor axis** and is 40 mm long.

Draw the given ellipse and complete the logo showing clearly all constructions.

3. The graphics show the basket of a child's pram.

Draw:

(a) An elevation in the direction of arrow **A**.

(b) An end view in the direction of arrow **B**.

(c) The complete **surface development** of the basket.

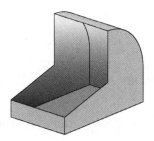

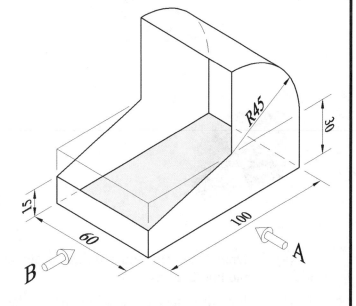

4.

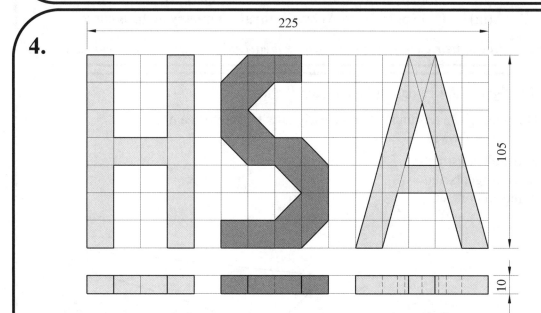

The figure shows the elevation and plan of the initials for the **H**ealth and **S**afety **A**uthority (**HSA**).

The grid in elevation is made up of 15 mm squares and the thickness in plan is 10 mm.

Draw **one** of the following views:
(a) An **isometric** view of the initials.

or

(b) An **oblique** view of the initials.

Note: The solution must be presented on standard drawing paper.

5. The graphics show the design of a logo for an Outdoor Adventure Centre.

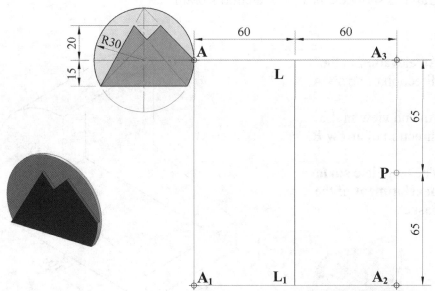

(a) Draw the given logo and then locate the points **A**, **A₁**, **A₂**, **A₃**, **P** and the line **L-L₁** as shown.

(b) Find the image of the given logo under the following transformations:

    (i) From point A to A₁ by a **translation**;

    (ii) From point A₁ to A₂ by an **axial symmetry** in the line **L-L₁**;

    (iii) From point A₂ to A₃ by a **central symmetry** in the point **P**.

Note: *All geometric constructions must be clearly shown on your drawing sheet.*

6. The figure shows a design for a motorbike logo.

Draw the given design showing clearly how to find the centres of the circles shown.

Show all construction lines, tangents and points of contact.

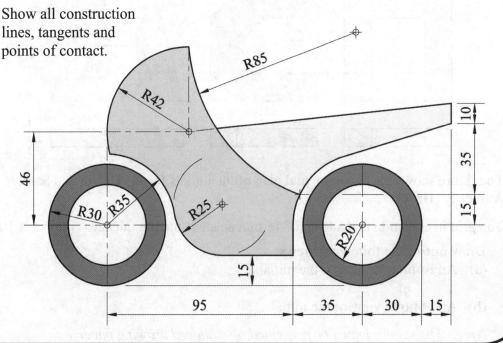

Coimisiún na Scrúduithe Stáit
State Examinations Commission

Junior Certificate Examination, 2014

Technical Graphics
Ordinary Level
Section A
(120 marks)

Monday, 16 June
Morning 9:30 - 12:00

2014 OL

Centre Number

Question	Mark
Section A	
1	
2	
3	
4	
5	
6	
TOTAL	
GRADE	

Instructions

(a) Answer **any ten** questions in the spaces provided.
All questions carry equal marks.

(b) Construction lines must be clearly shown.

(c) All measurements are in millimetres.

(d) This booklet must be handed up at the end of the examination.

(e) Write your examination number in the box provided below
and on all other pages used.

Examination Number:

1. Shown is the elevation and **incomplete** end view of a data projector. Also shown is a 3D graphic of the projector.

Insert the missing lines in the end view.

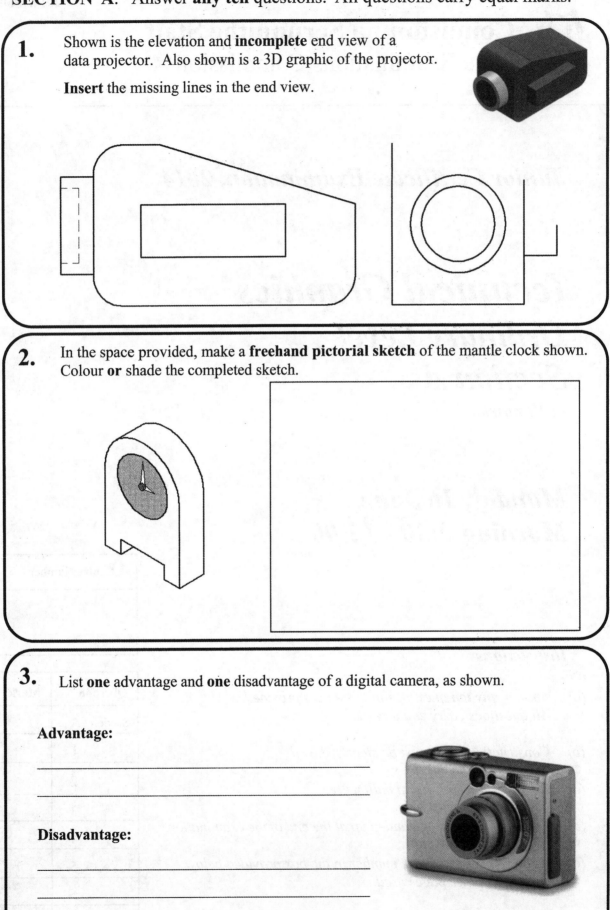

2. In the space provided, make a **freehand pictorial sketch** of the mantle clock shown. Colour **or** shade the completed sketch.

3. List **one** advantage and **one** disadvantage of a digital camera, as shown.

Advantage:

_____

_____

Disadvantage:

_____

_____

4. **Fig. 1** shows a webcam logo inscribed in the square **ABCD**.

Draw the enlarged logo in the given square **ABCD** in **Fig. 2**.

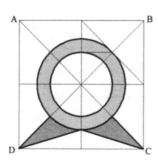

Fig. 1

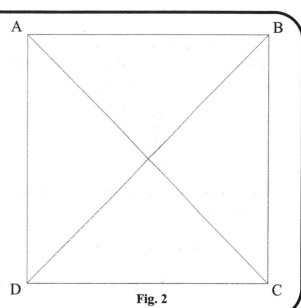

Fig. 2

---

5. **Fig. 1** shows a curling stone and handle. The line **PL** is a tangent to the ellipse at **P**. Locate the focal points of the ellipse in **Fig. 2** and complete the handle of the curling stone by drawing the tangent **PL**.

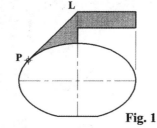

Fig. 1

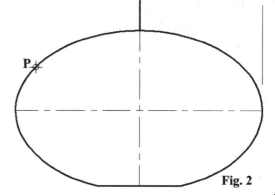

Fig. 2

---

6. The elevation and plan of a measuring tape are shown.

Make a well proportioned **freehand sketch** of the measuring tape in the space provided.

Colour **or** shade the completed sketch.

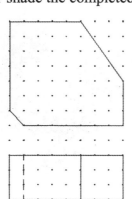

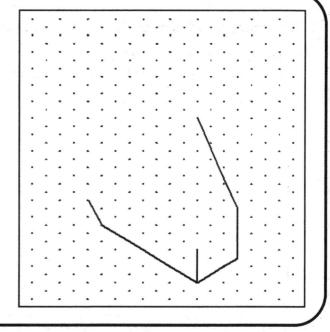

7. The outline of an ink cartridge is shown.
Also shown is a 3D graphic of the cartridge.

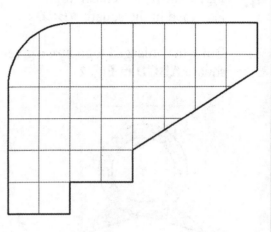

Write down the area of the ink cartridge in square units.

1 square = 1 square unit.

Area of the cartridge: _____ **square units**.

8. Using the scale provided, **measure** and **write down** the dimensions **A** and **B** for the games-console camera shown.

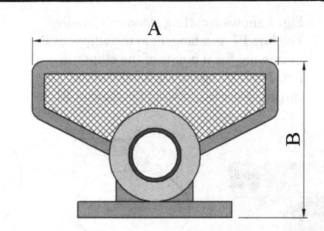

A: _____

B: _____

9. The figure shows a set of blocks.
Draw, in the space provided, an elevation of the blocks in the direction of the arrow.

154

10. The drawing shows the outline of a wrench.

The centres of the arcs and one point of contact are shown.

Show clearly the remaining points of contact.

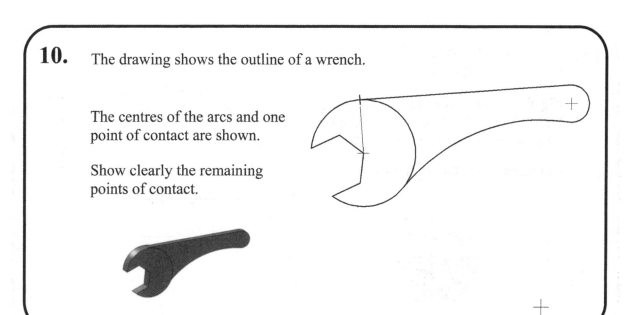

11. Write down **any two** CAD commands used to produce the drawing of the garden seat.

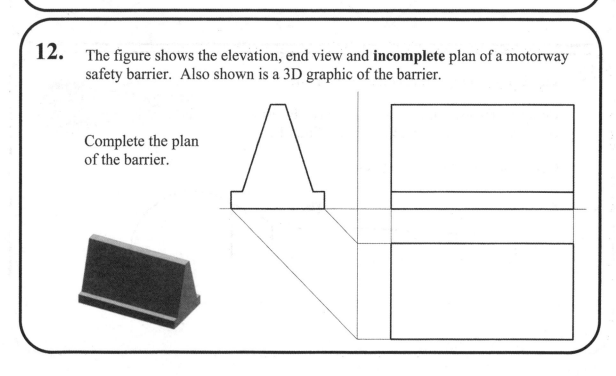

Any **two** CAD commands: _____

_____

12. The figure shows the elevation, end view and **incomplete** plan of a motorway safety barrier. Also shown is a 3D graphic of the barrier.

Complete the plan of the barrier.

13. **Fig. 1** shows the design of a logo for a bakery. The logo is based on a semi-hexagon.

Fig. 2 shows an **incomplete** view of the logo. Complete the logo by drawing the semi-hexagon. Show all constructions.

Colour **or** shade the completed logo.

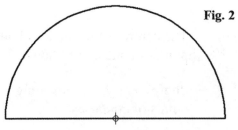

Fig. 2

Fig. 1

14. The figure shows an **incomplete** two point perspective drawing of a couch. A small 3D graphic of the couch is also shown.
Complete the perspective drawing of the couch.

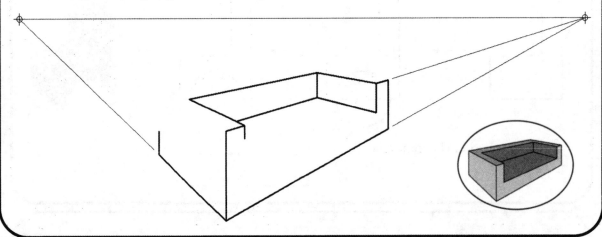

15. **Fig. 1** shows a logo based on a microphone.

Complete the logo of the microphone in **Fig. 2** by constructing an axial symmetry in the line **LL₁**.

Colour **or** shade the completed logo.

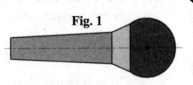

Fig. 1

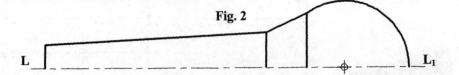

Fig. 2

L   L₁

Coimisiún na Scrúduithe Stáit
State Examinations Commission

2014. S60B

Junior Certificate Examination, 2014

Technical Graphics
Ordinary Level
Section B
(280 marks)

Monday, 16 June
Morning 9:30 - 12:00

2014 OL

Instructions

(a) Answer **any four** questions. All questions carry equal marks.

(b) The number of the question must be distinctly marked by the side of each answer.

(c) Work on **one side** of the answer paper only.

(d) Write your examination number on each sheet of paper used.

SECTION B. Answer **any four** questions. All questions carry equal marks.

1. The graphics show a design for a stapler.

Draw:

(a) An elevation in the direction of arrow **A**.

(b) A plan projected from the elevation.

(c) Insert **any four** dimensions.

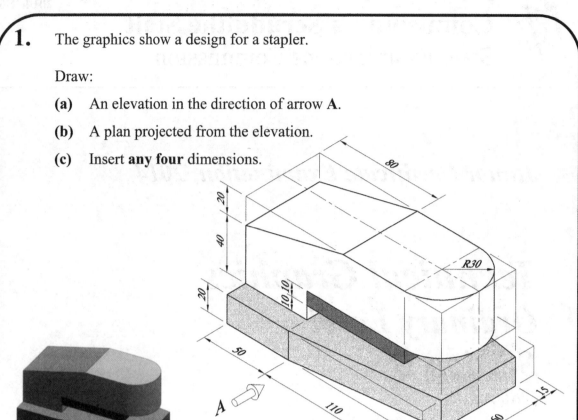

2. The graphics show the logo for the **SUPERUGBY** league. The logo is based on circles and on an ellipse as shown.

The curve **ABCD** is elliptical. **AC** is the **major axis** of the ellipse and is 120 mm long. **OB** is half the **minor axis** and is 40 mm long.

Draw the given ellipse and complete the logo showing clearly all constructions.

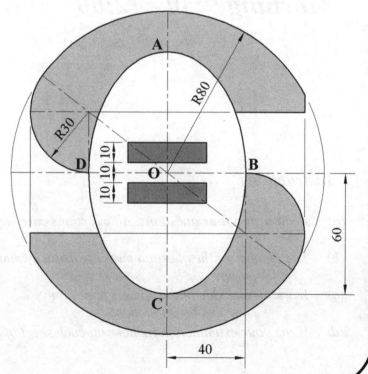

3. The graphics show a holder for a lifebuoy.

Draw:
(a) An elevation in the direction of arrow **A**.

(b) An end view in the direction of arrow **B**.

(c) The complete **surface development** of the lifebuoy holder.

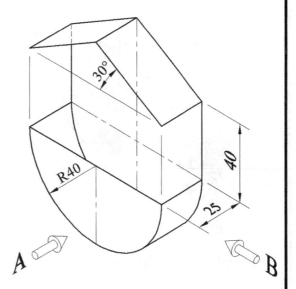

4.

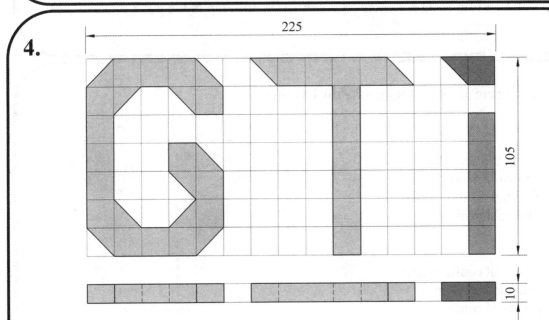

The figure shows the elevation and plan of the initials **GTi** used by many car companies.

The grid in elevation is made up of 15 mm squares and the thickness in plan is 10 mm.

Draw **one** of the following views:
(a) An **isometric** view of the initials.

or

(b) An **oblique** view of the initials.

Note: The solution must be presented on standard drawing paper.

5.

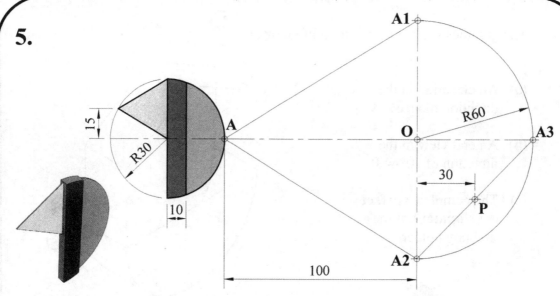

The graphics show the design of a logo for a golf society.

(a)   Draw the given logo and then locate the points **A, O, A1, A2, A3** and **P** as shown.

(b)   Find the image of the given logo under the following transformations:

      (i)   From point A to A1 by a **translation**;

      (ii)   From point A1 to A2 by an **axial symmetry** in the line **A-A3**;

      (iii)   From point A2 to A3 by a **central symmetry** in the point **P**.

---

6.   The figure shows a design for a toy hammer.

Draw the given design showing clearly how to find the centres of the circles shown.

Show all construction lines, tangents and points of contact.

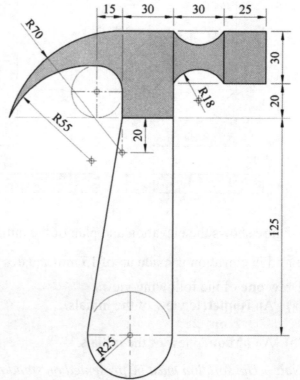

Coimisiún na Scrúduithe Stáit
State Examinations Commission

Junior Certificate Examination, 2013

Technical Graphics
Ordinary Level
Section A
(120 marks)

Monday, 17 June
Morning 9:30 - 12:00

Instructions

(a) Answer **any ten** questions in the spaces provided.
All questions carry equal marks.

(b) Construction lines must be clearly shown.

(c) All measurements are in millimetres.

(d) This booklet must be handed up at the end of the examination.

(e) Write your examination number in the box provided below
and on all other pages used.

Examination Number:

Centre Number

Question	Mark
Section A	
1	
2	
3	
4	
5	
6	
TOTAL	
GRADE	

2013 OL

1. Shown is the elevation and **incomplete** end view of a plug top. Also shown is a 3D graphic of the plug top. **Insert** the missing lines in the end view.

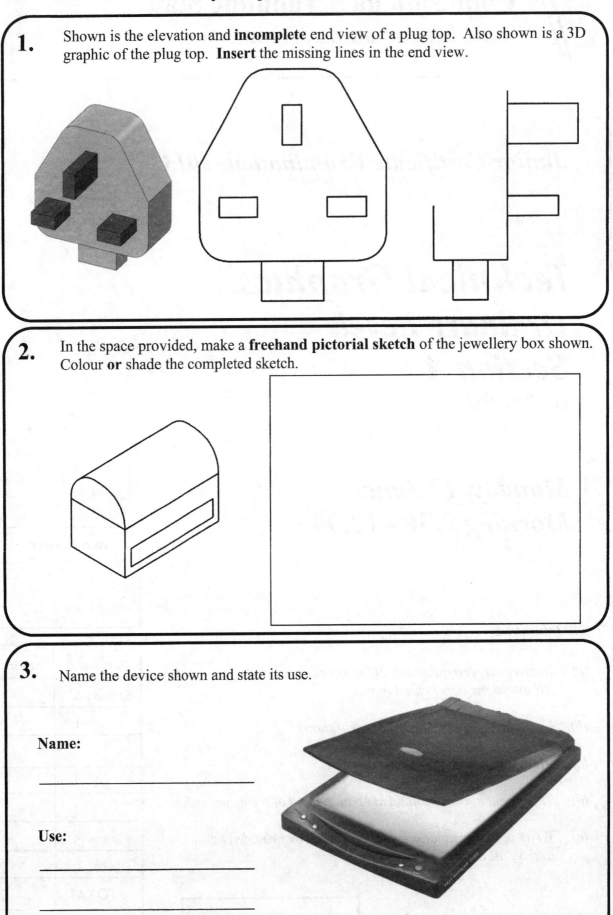

2. In the space provided, make a **freehand pictorial sketch** of the jewellery box shown. Colour **or** shade the completed sketch.

3. Name the device shown and state its use.

Name:

_____

Use:

_____

4. **Fig. 1** shows a media player logo inscribed in a square **ABCD**.

Draw the enlarged logo in the given square **ABCD** in **Fig. 2**.

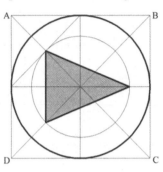

Fig. 1

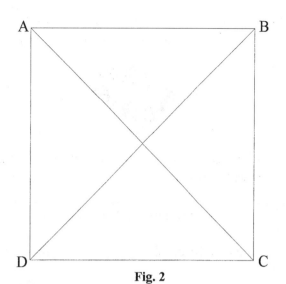

Fig. 2

5. **Fig. 1** shows the design of a presentation pointer based on an ellipse and a circle. **F** and **F₁** are the focal points of the ellipse. Locate the focal points in **Fig. 2** and complete the design by drawing the shape **AF₁BF**.

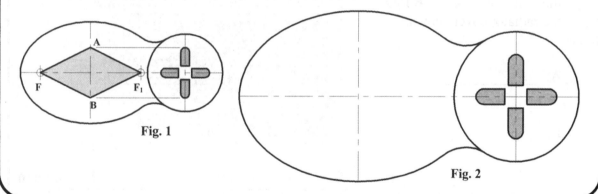

Fig. 1

Fig. 2

6. The elevation and plan of an awards podium are shown.

Make a well proportioned **freehand sketch** of the podium in the space provided.

Colour **or** shade the completed sketch.

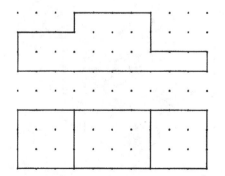

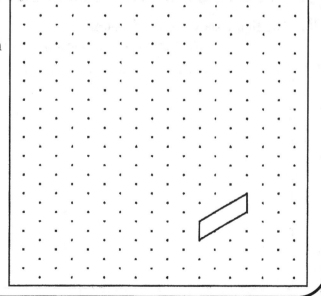

7. The outline of a memory card is shown. Also shown is a 3D graphic of the card.

Write down the area of the memory card in square units.

1 square = 1 square unit.

Area of the card: _____ **square units**.

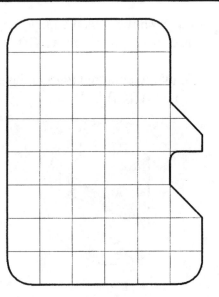

8. Using the scale provided, **measure** and **write down** the dimensions **A** and **B** for the radiator cover shown.

A: _____

B: _____

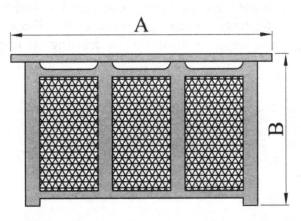

9. The figure shows a set of blocks.
Draw, in the space provided, the elevation of the blocks in the direction of the arrow.

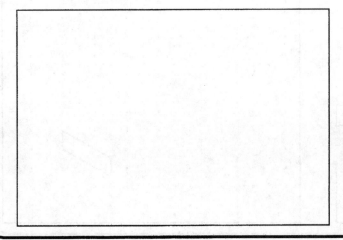

164

10. The figure shows the incomplete outline of a chess piece of symmetrical design. Also shown is a 3D graphic of the chess piece.

Complete the drawing of the chess piece showing all constructions and points of contact.

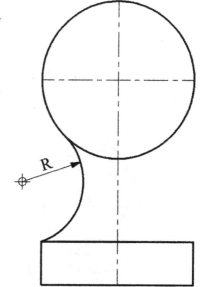

11. List the CAD commands used to produce the drawing of the bookend from **A** to **B** and **B** to **C**.

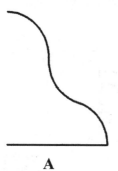

| A | B | C |

Commands: A ⟶ B _____ B ⟶ C _____

12. The graphics show a computer speaker.

Draw the **shadow** cast by the speaker shown in **Fig. 1** when the light source is parallel to the direction of the arrow.

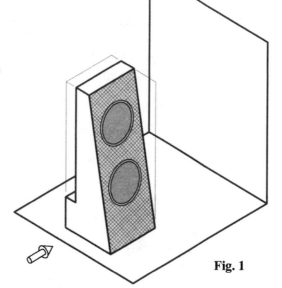

Fig. 1

13. Fig. 1 shows a view of a watch based on a pentagon.

Fig. 2 shows an **incomplete** view of the watch. Complete the view by drawing the regular pentagon. Show all construction.

Fig. 1

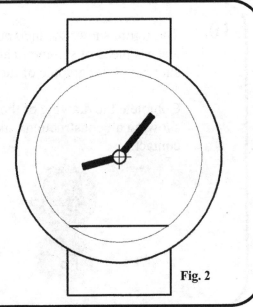

Fig. 2

14. The figure shows an **incomplete** two point perspective drawing of a microwave oven. A small 3D graphic of the oven is also shown. Complete the perspective drawing of the oven.

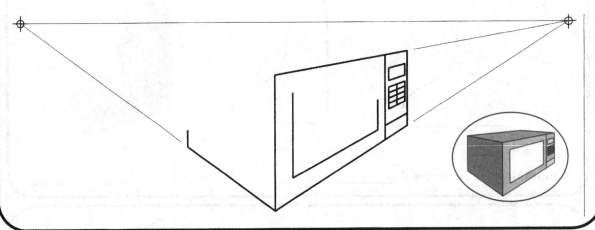

15. Fig. 1 shows the design of a shipping logo.

Complete the logo in **Fig. 2** by constructing an axial symmetry in the line **LL₁**.

Colour **or** shade the completed logo.

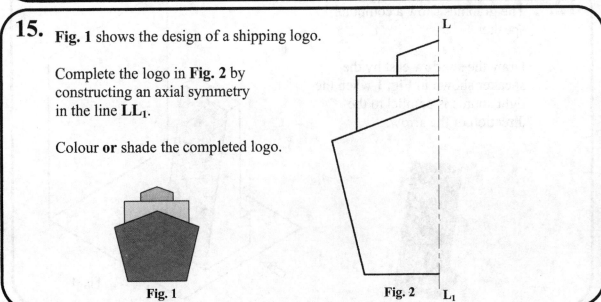

Fig. 1

Fig. 2 L₁

166

2013. S60B

Coimisiún na Scrúduithe Stáit
State Examinations Commission

Junior Certificate Examination, 2013

Technical Graphics
Ordinary Level
Section B
(280 marks)

Monday, 17 June
Morning 9:30 - 12:00

2013 OL

Instructions

(a) Answer **any four** questions. All questions carry equal marks.

(b) The number of the question must be distinctly marked by the side of each answer.

(c) Work on **one side** of the answer paper only.

(d) Write your examination number on each sheet of paper used.

SECTION B. Answer **any four** questions. All questions carry equal marks.

1. The graphics show a design for a **golf putting aid**.

Draw:

(a) An elevation in the direction of arrow **A**.

(b) A plan projected from the elevation.

(c) Insert **any four** dimensions.

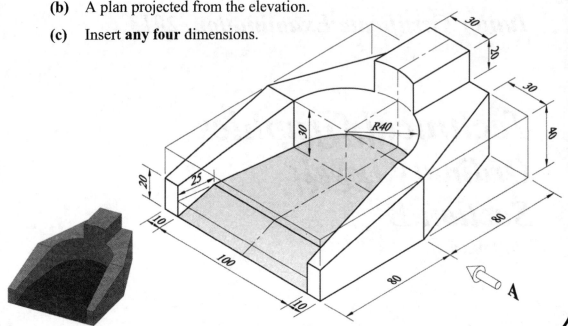

2. The graphics show a logo for a phone app (application). The app gives restaurant reviews and the logo is based on semi-circles and an ellipse as shown.

The curve **ABCD** is elliptical. **AC** is the **major axis** of the ellipse and is 100 mm long. **OB** is half the **minor axis** and is 35 mm long.

Draw the given ellipse and complete the logo showing clearly all construction.

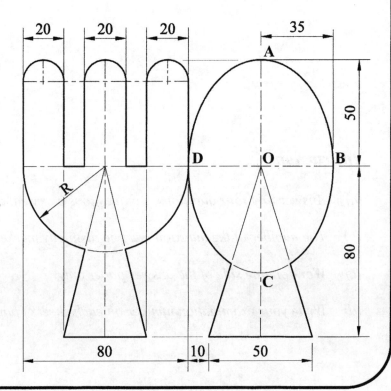

3. The graphics show a design for a telephone booth.

Draw:
(a) An elevation in the direction of arrow **A**.

(b) An end view in the direction of arrow **B**.

(c) The complete **surface development** of the telephone booth.

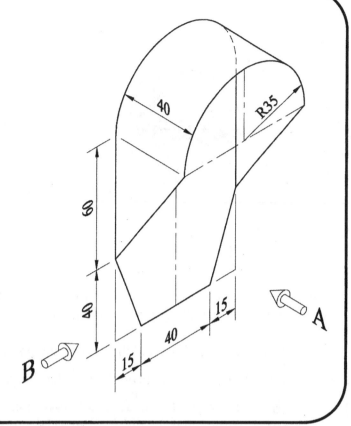

4.

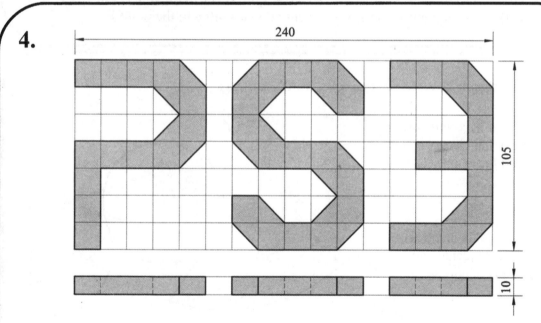

The figure shows the elevation and plan of a logo for a **games console - PS3**.
The grid in elevation is made up of 15mm squares and the thickness in plan is 10mm.

Draw **one** of the following views:
(a) An **isometric** view of the initials.

or

(b) An **oblique** view of the initials.

Note: The solution must be presented on standard drawing paper.

5.

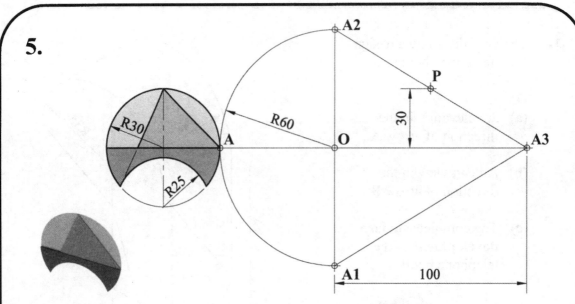

The given figure shows the design of a logo for a boating club.
Also shown is a small 3D graphic of the logo.

(a) Draw the given logo and then locate the points **A**, **A1**, **A2**, **A3**, **O** and **P** as shown.

(b) Find the image of the given logo under the following transformations:

(i) From point A to A1 by a **translation**;
(ii) From point A1 to A2 by an **axial symmetry** in the line **A-A3**;
(iii) From point A2 to A3 by a **central symmetry** in the point **P**.

6. The figure shows the design for a child's toy duck.

Draw the given design, showing clearly how to find the centres of the circles shown.

Show all construction lines, tangents and points of contact.

Note: *Choose your own dimensions for the eye of the duck.*

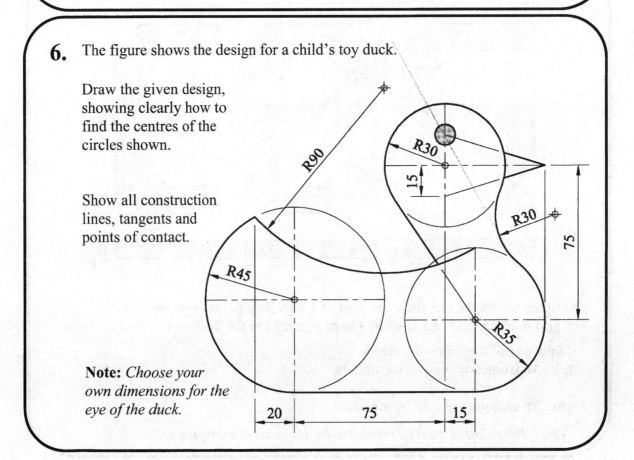

Coimisiún na Scrúduithe Stáit
State Examinations Commission

Junior Certificate Examination, 2012

Technical Graphics
Ordinary Level
Section A
(120 marks)

Monday, 18 June
Morning 9:30 - 12:00

Centre Number

Instructions

(a) Answer **any ten** questions in the spaces provided.
All questions carry equal marks.

(b) Construction lines must be clearly shown.

(c) All measurements are in millimetres.

(d) This booklet must be handed up at the end of the examination.

(e) Write your examination number in the box provided below
and on all other pages used.

Examination Number:

Question	Mark
Section A	
1	
2	
3	
4	
5	
6	
TOTAL	
GRADE	

2012 OL

SECTION A.   Answer **any ten** questions. All questions carry equal marks.

1 Shown is the **incomplete** elevation and **incomplete** end view of a writing desk.

Also shown is a 3D graphic of the desk.

Insert the missing lines in both the elevation and the end view.

2 In the space provided, make a **freehand sketch** of the wastepaper bin shown. Colour **or** shade the completed sketch.

3 List **one** advantage and **one** disadvantage of a tablet computer, as shown.

Advantage:

_____

_____

_____

Disadvantage:

_____

_____

_____

4 **Fig.1** shows a design for a speaker inscribed in the square **ABCD**.

Draw an enlarged design of the speaker in the given square **ABCD** in **Fig. 2**.

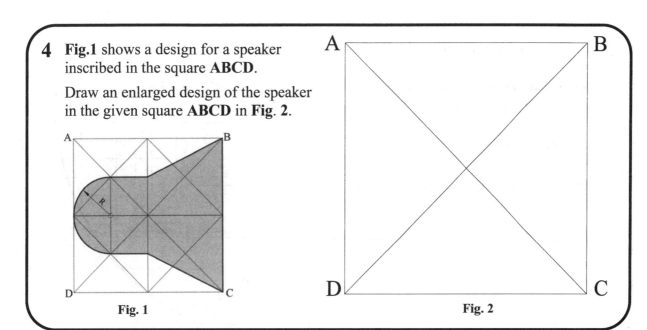

Fig. 1

Fig. 2

5 **Fig.1** shows the design of a helmet based on a semi-ellipse with an attached safety shield. The line **PL** is a tangent to the semi-ellipse at **P**. Locate the focal points of the semi-ellipse in **Fig.2** and complete the design by drawing the tangent **PL**.

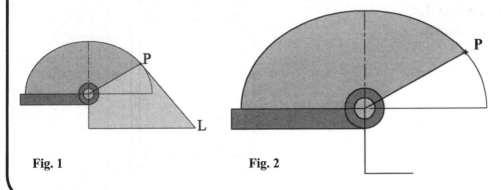

Fig. 1   Fig. 2

6 The elevation and plan of a garden seat are shown. Complete the given 3D sketch of the seat on the grid provided. Colour **or** shade the completed sketch.

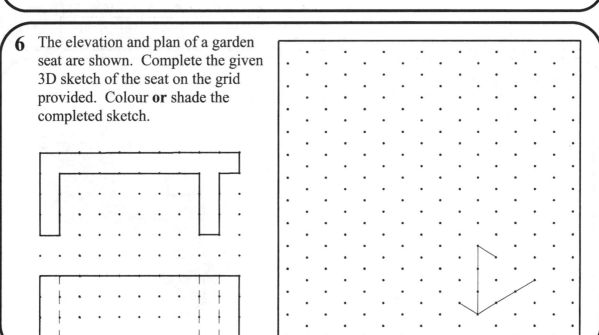

7 The design of a sports trophy is shown.

Write down the area of the trophy in square centimetres - cm^2.

1 square = 1 cm^2

Area of the trophy: _____ cm^2.

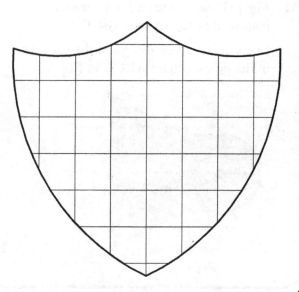

8 Using the scale provided, **measure** and **write down** the dimensions **A** and **B** of the clothes stand shown.

A: _____

B: _____

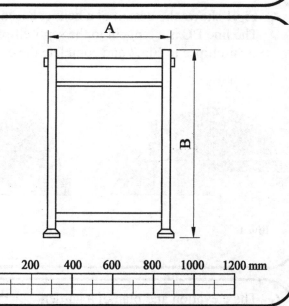

9 The figure shows a set of blocks.
Draw, in the space provided, an elevation of the blocks in the direction of the arrow.

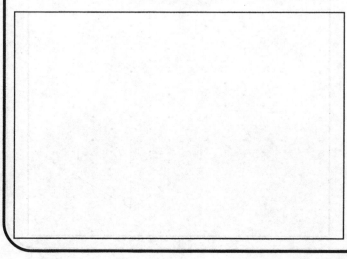

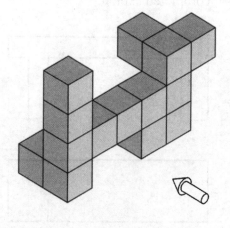

10 The drawing shows the design of a light bulb.

Show clearly all the points of contact between the arcs.

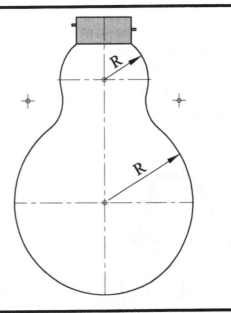

11 List the CAD commands used to produce the figures **A** to **B** and **B** to **C**.

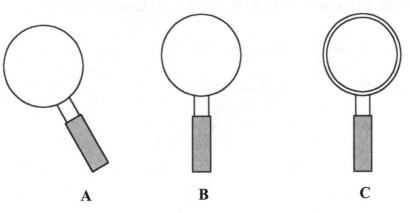

| A | B | C |

Commands: A ⟶ B _____   B ⟶ C _____

12 The graphic shows a small table lamp.
Draw the **shadow** cast by the base of the lamp shown in **Fig.1** when the direction of light is parallel to the arrow.

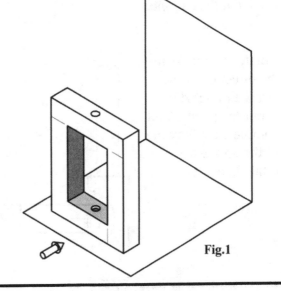

Fig.1

13 **Fig.1** shows the design of a road sign based on a circle and a regular hexagon.

Complete **Fig. 2** to show the design of the road sign.

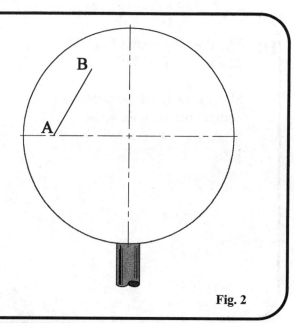
Fig. 2

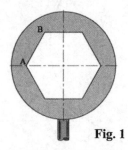
Fig. 1

14 The figure shows an incomplete perspective drawing of a toaster.
A small 3D graphic of the toaster is also shown. Complete the perspective drawing.

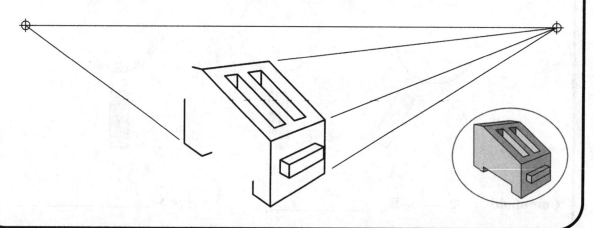

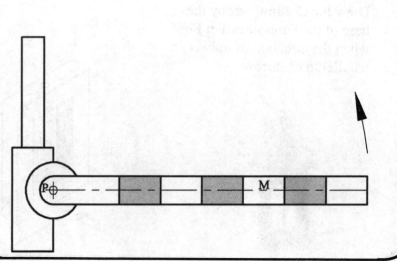

15 The diagram shows a barrier at the entrance to a car park.

Rotate the arm **M** in the direction of the arrow through 45° about the point **P** and complete the drawing of the arm in the rotated position.

Coimisiún na Scrúduithe Stáit
State Examinations Commission

2012. S60B

Junior Certificate Examination, 2012

Technical Graphics
Ordinary Level
Section B
(280 marks)

Monday, 18 June
Morning 9:30 - 12:00

Instructions

*(a) Answer **any four** questions. All questions carry equal marks.*

(b) The number of the question must be distinctly marked by the side of each answer.

*(c) Work on **one side** of the answer paper only.*

(d) Write your examination number on each sheet of paper used.

2012 OL

SECTION B. Answer **any four** questions. All questions carry equal marks.

1 The figure shows a design for a letterbox.

Draw:

(a) An elevation in the direction of arrow **A**.

(b) An end elevation in the direction of arrow **B**.

(c) Insert **any four** dimensions.

Note:
The back surface S is vertical as shown.

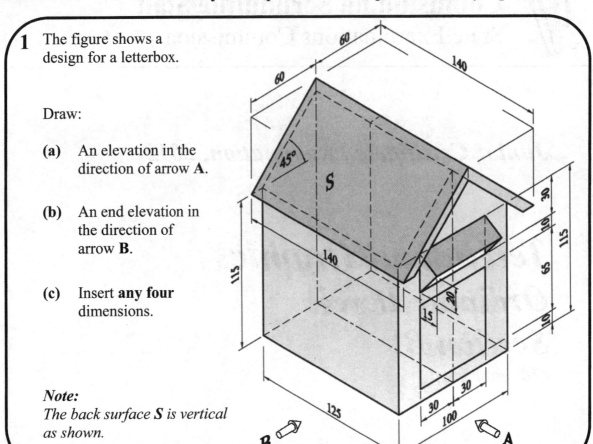

2 The figure shows the design of a logo for a locksmith.
The curve **ABC** is a semi-ellipse. **AC** is the **major axis**, **OB** is half the **minor axis** and is 50 mm long as shown.
Draw the given logo showing clearly all construction lines.

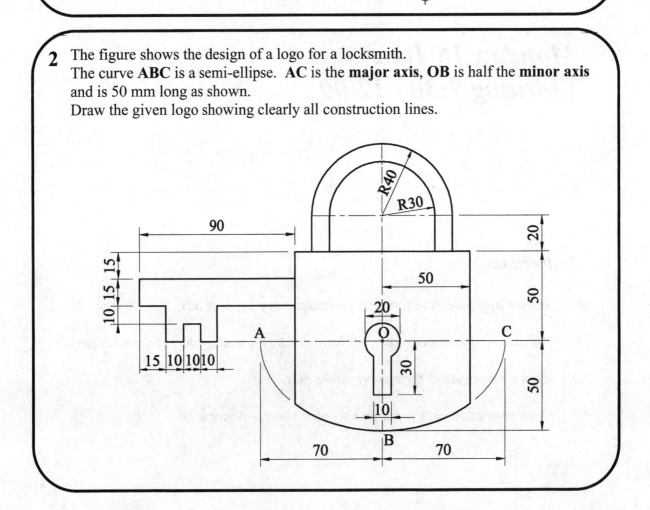

3 The figure shows a design for a cup-holder. Also shown is a 3D graphic of the cup-holder.

Draw:

(a) An elevation in the direction of arrow **A**.

(b) A plan projected from the elevation.

(c) The complete **surface development** of the cup-holder.

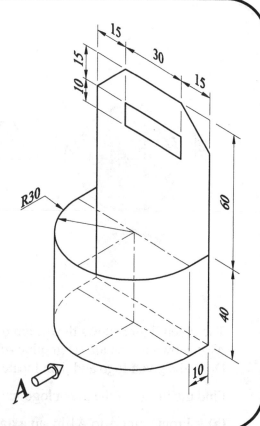

4

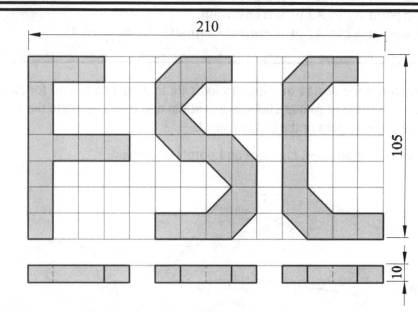

The figure shows the elevation and plan of the initials for the **F**orest **S**tewardship **C**ouncil (**FSC**). The Forest Stewardship Council promotes the responsible management of the world's forests.

The grid in elevation is made up of 15 mm squares and the thickness in plan is 10 mm.

Draw **one** of the following views:
(a) An **isometric** view of the initials

or

(b) An **oblique** view of the initials.

Note: The solution must be presented on standard drawing paper.

5

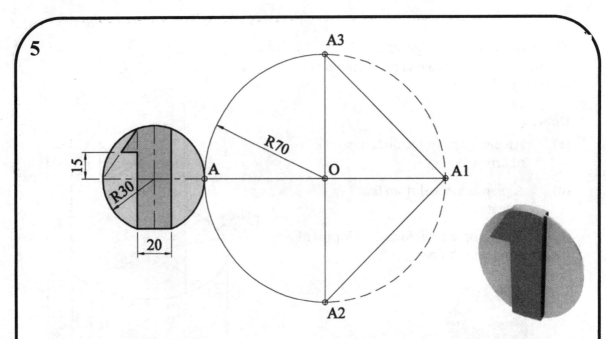

The given figure shows the design of a logo for a television channel - Channel **1**.
Also shown is a small 3D graphic of the logo.
Draw the given logo and then locate the points **A**, **A1**, **A2**, **A3** and **O** as shown.

Find the image of the given logo under the following transformations:

(a) From point A to A1 by an **axial symmetry** in the line **A2-A3**;
(b) From point A1 to A2 by a **translation**;
(c) From point A2 to A3 by a **central symmetry** in the point **O**.

6 The figure shows the design of a logo to indicate that an area is safe for swimming.
Draw the semi-circle of radius 100 mm as shown and then complete the given logo.
The line **LM** is a tangent to the circle from **L**.

Show all construction lines, tangents and points of contact.

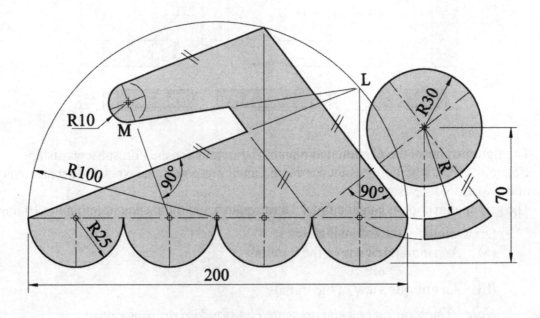

Coimisiún na Scrúduithe Stáit
State Examinations Commission

Junior Certificate Examination, 2011

Technical Graphics
Ordinary Level
Section A
(120 marks)

Monday, 20 June
Morning 9:30 - 12:00

Instructions

(a) Answer **any ten** questions in the spaces provided.
All questions carry equal marks.

(b) Construction lines must be clearly shown.

(c) All measurements are in millimetres.

(d) This booklet must be handed up at the end of the examination.

(e) Write your examination number in the box provided below
and on all other pages used.

Examination Number:

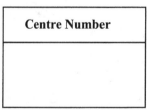

Centre Number	

Question	Mark
Section A	
1	
2	
3	
4	
5	
6	
TOTAL	
GRADE	

2011 OL

SECTION A. Answer **any ten** questions. All questions carry equal marks.

1 The **incomplete** elevation and the end view of a post box are shown. Also shown is a 3D graphic of the post box. **Insert** the missing lines in the elevation.

POST

POST

2 In the space provided, make a **freehand sketch** of the toolbox shown. Colour **or** shade the completed sketch.

3 Name the computer components labelled **A** and **B** and give one use for each.

A: _____

Use _____

_____

B: _____

Use _____

_____

182

4 **Fig.1** shows a logo for a restaurant inscribed in the square **ABCD**.

Draw the enlarged logo in the given square **ABCD** in **Fig. 2**.

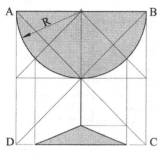

Fig. 1

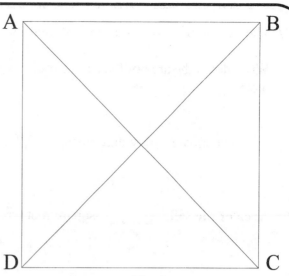

Fig. 2

5 **Fig.1** shows the design of a computer mouse based on an ellipse and two arcs.
F1 is a focal point of the ellipse and is also the centre for the arc **AOB**.
Locate the focal point **F1** in **Fig. 2** and complete the design by drawing the arc **AOB**.

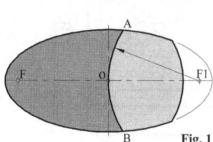

Fig. 1

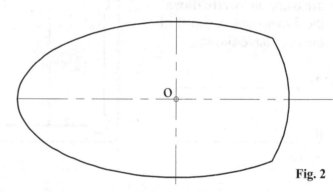

Fig. 2

6 The elevation and plan of a bridge are shown. Complete the given sketch of the bridge on the grid provided. Colour **or** shade the completed sketch.

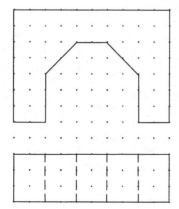

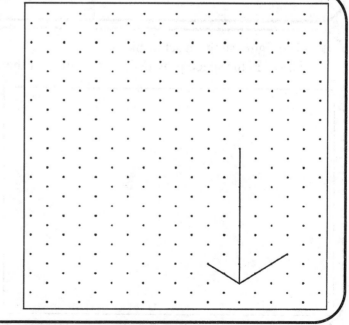

7 The outline of a boat and sail is shown.

Write down the area of the sail in square metres.

1 square = 1 square metre.

Area of the sail: _____ square metres.

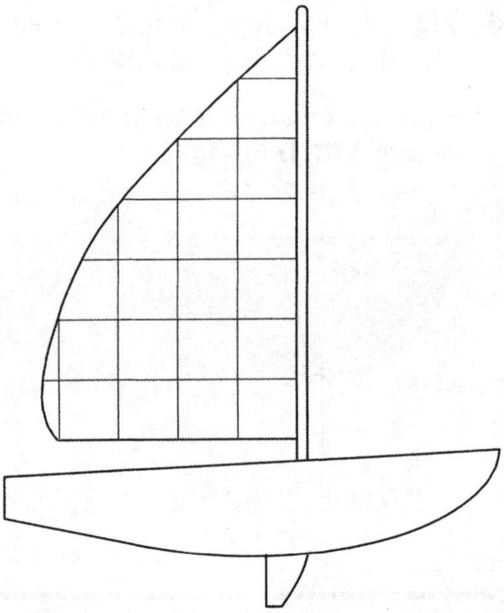

8 Using the scale provided, **measure** and **write down** the dimensions **A** and **B** of the pool table shown.

A: _____

B: _____

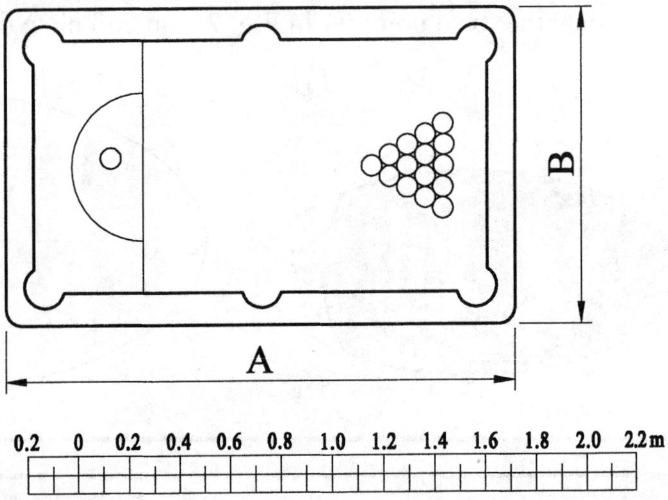

9 The figure shows a set of blocks.
Draw, in the space provided, an elevation of the blocks in the direction of the arrow.

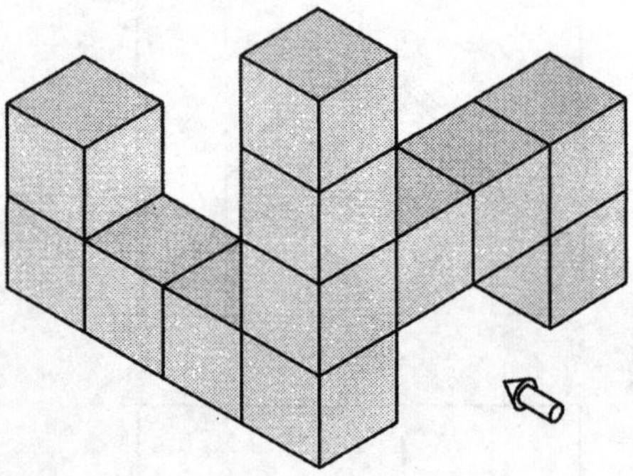

10 The drawing shows the outline of a piano.

Show clearly the points of contact between the circles **A**, **B** and **C**.

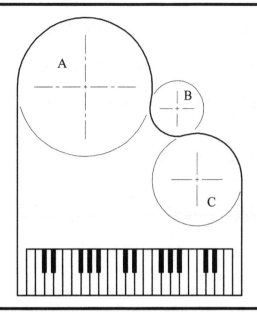

11 List the CAD commands used to produce the figures **A** to **B** and **B** to **C**.

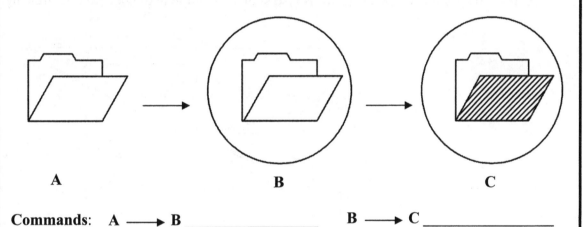

Commands: A ⟶ B _____   B ⟶ C _____

12 Draw the **shadow** cast by the clock when the direction of light is parallel to the arrow.

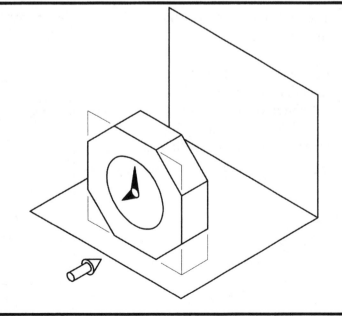

13 The figure shows a small weighing scales.

   (a) Name the shape of the base **A**.

   (b) Write down the size of the angle **B**.

   Shape of base **A**: _____

   Size of angle **B**: _____

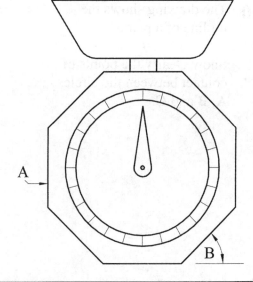

14 The figure shows an incomplete perspective drawing of a data projector.
A small 3D graphic of the projector is also shown. Complete the perspective drawing.

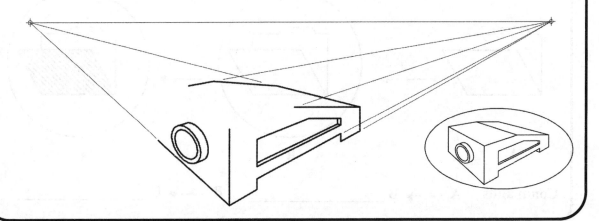

15 The diagram shows a design for a door handle.

Rotate the lever **L** in the direction of the arrow through 30° about the point **P** and complete the drawing of the lever in the rotated position.

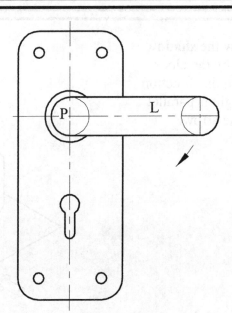

2011. S60B

Coimisiún na Scrúduithe Stáit
State Examinations Commission

Junior Certificate Examination, 2011

Technical Graphics
Ordinary Level
Section B
(280 marks)

Monday, 20 June
Morning 9:30 - 12:00

Instructions

(a) Answer **any four** questions. All questions carry equal marks.

(b) The number of the question must be distinctly marked by the side of each answer.

(c) Work on **one side** of the answer paper only.

(d) Write your examination number on each sheet of paper used.

2011 OL

1 The figure shows the outline of an MP3 player and docking station.

Also shown is a 3D graphic of the MP3 player and docking station.

Draw:

(a) An elevation in the direction of arrow **A**.

(b) An end elevation in the direction of arrow **B**.

Insert **any four** dimensions.

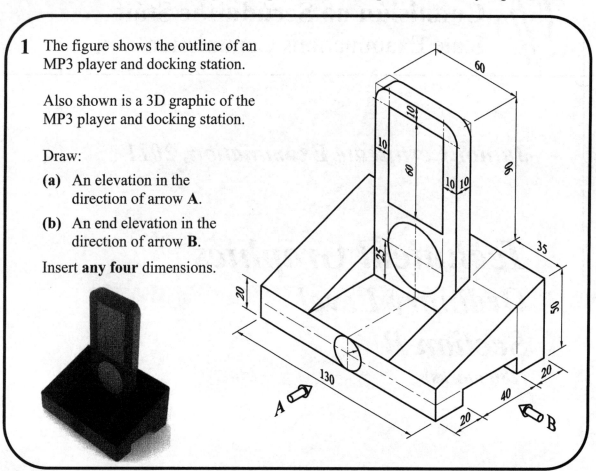

2

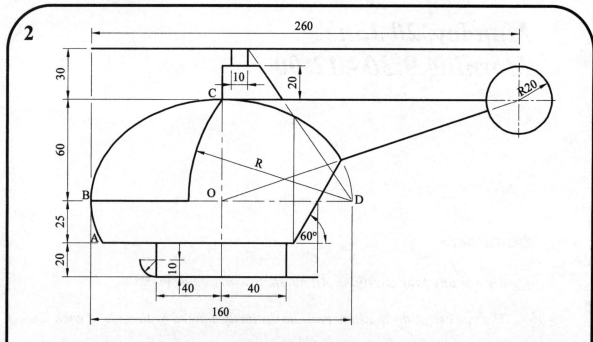

The figure shows the design of a model helicopter.
The curve **ABCD** is elliptical. **BD** is the **major axis** of the ellipse and is 160 mm long.
OC is half the **minor axis** and is 60 mm long as shown.

Draw the given portion of the ellipse and then complete the drawing of the helicopter.
Show all construction lines.

3

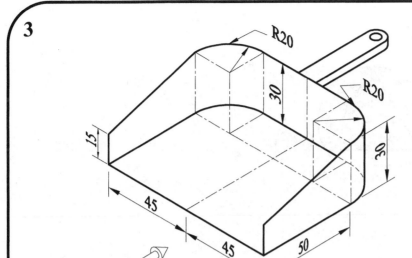

The figure shows a design for a dustpan. Also shown is a 3D graphic of the dustpan.

Draw: **(a)** An elevation in the direction of arrow **A**.

(b) A plan projected from the elevation.

(c) The complete **surface development** of the dustpan.

Note: Ignore the handle of the dustpan in all your drawings.

4

Every new house must have a **B**uilding **E**nergy **R**ating - **BER** - certificate.
The figure shows the elevation and plan of the initials **BER**.
The grid in elevation is made up of 15 mm squares and the thickness in plan is 10 mm.

Draw **one** of the following views:
(a) An **isometric** view of the initials

or

(b) An **oblique** view of the initials.

Note: The solution must be presented on standard drawing paper.

5

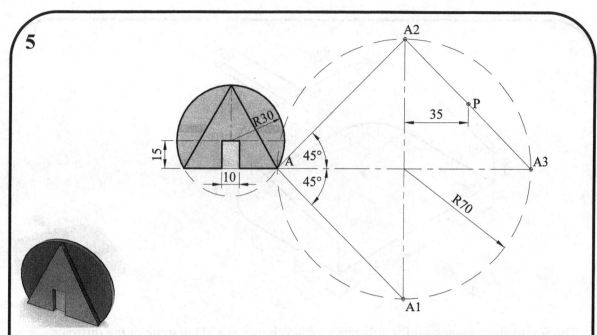

The given figure shows the design of a logo for a camp site. Also shown is a small 3D graphic of the logo.

Draw the given logo and then locate the points **A**, **A1**, **A2**, **A3** and **P** as shown.

Find the image of the given figure under the following transformations:

(a) From point A to A1 by a **translation**.
(b) From point A1 to A2 by an **axial symmetry** in the line **A-A3**.
(c) From point A2 to A3 by a **central symmetry** in the point **P**.

6 The figure shows a design for the body of a guitar.

Draw the given design, showing clearly how to find the centres of the circles shown.

Show all construction lines, tangents and points of contact.

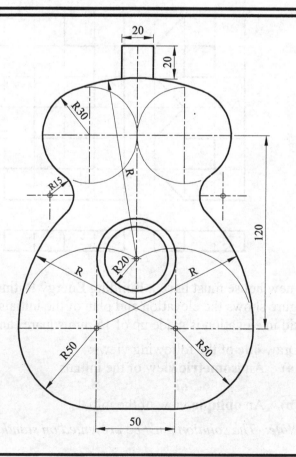

Coimisiún na Scrúduithe Stáit
State Examinations Commission

Junior Certificate Examination, 2010

Technical Graphics
Ordinary Level
Section A
(120 marks)

Monday, 21 June
Morning 9:30 - 12:00

Centre Number

Instructions

(a) Answer **any ten** questions in the spaces provided.
All questions carry equal marks.

(b) Construction lines must be clearly shown.

(c) All measurements are in millimetres.

(d) This booklet must be handed up at the end of the examination.

(e) Write your examination number in the box provided below
and on all other pages used.

Examination Number:

Question	Mark
Section A	
1	
2	
3	
4	
5	
6	
TOTAL	
GRADE	

2010 OL

SECTION A. Answer **any ten** questions. All questions carry equal marks.

1 Shown is an **incomplete elevation**, the plan and end view of a calculator. Also shown is a 3D graphic of the calculator.

Insert the missing lines in the elevation.

2 In the space provided, make a **freehand sketch** of the sports bottle shown. Colour **or** shade the completed sketch.

3 **Name** the computer device shown and state its use.

Name: _____ Use: _____

192

4 Draw a line from **C** which will divide the area of the triangle **ABC** into two equal parts.

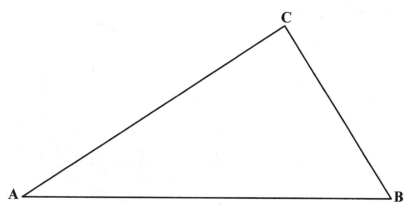

5 **Fig. 1** shows the design of a clock based on an ellipse and a circle. In **Fig. 2**, **F** and **F1** are the focal points of the ellipse. The lines **LM** and **LN** are tangents to the ellipse.

Locate point **N** and complete **Fig. 2** by drawing the tangents **LM** and **LN**.

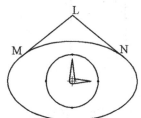

Fig. 1

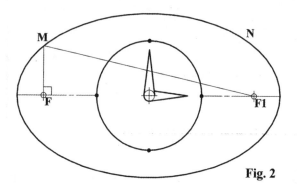

Fig. 2

6 The outline of a lens from a pair of reading glasses is shown on the grid below. Also shown is a 3D graphic of the reading glasses. Write down the area of the lens in square units.

1 square = 1 square unit

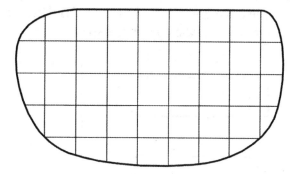

Area of lens: _____ square units

2010 OL

7 The figure shows a set of blocks.
Draw, in the space provided, an elevation of the blocks in the direction of the arrow.

8 Using the scale provided, **measure** and **write down** the dimensions **A** and **B** of the fireplace shown.

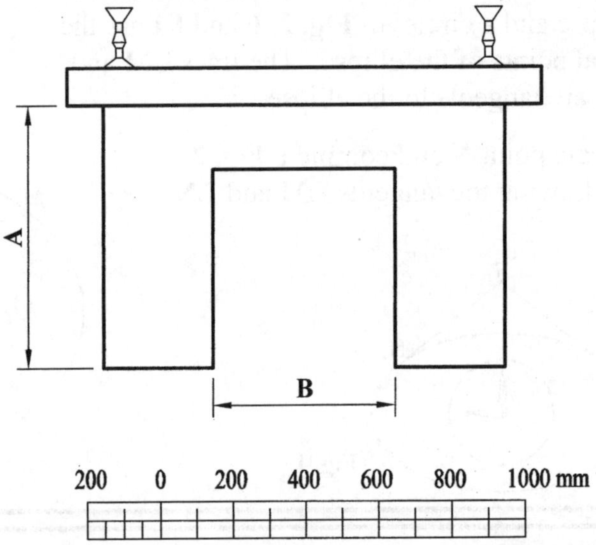

A: _____

B: _____

200   0   200   400   600   800   1000 mm

9 Shown is the elevation, plan and incomplete isometric view of an USB drive.
Complete the given sketch of the USB drive on the grid provided.
Colour **or** shade the completed sketch.

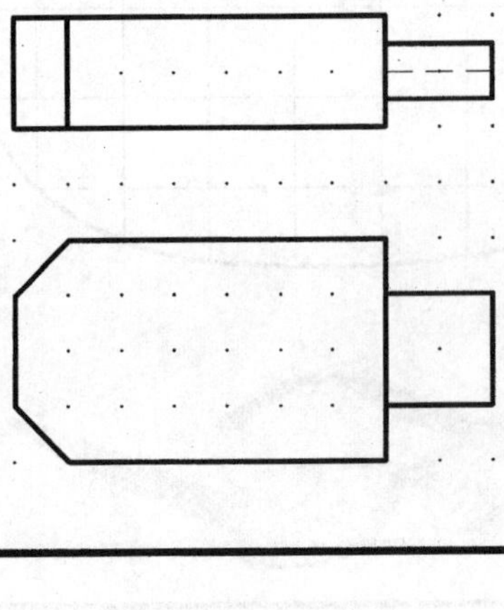

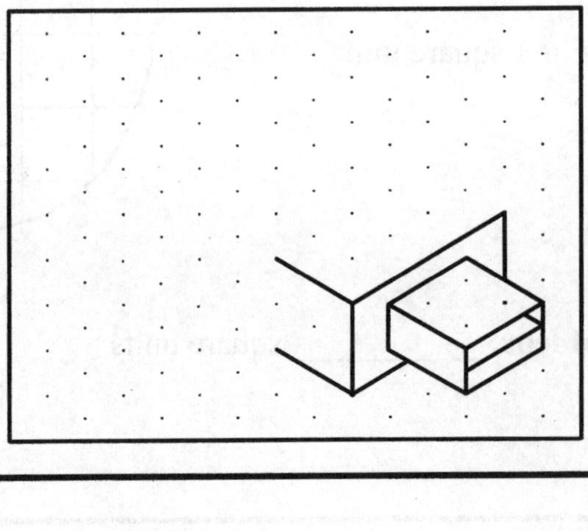

10 List the CAD commands used to produce the figures **A** to **B** and **B** to **C**.

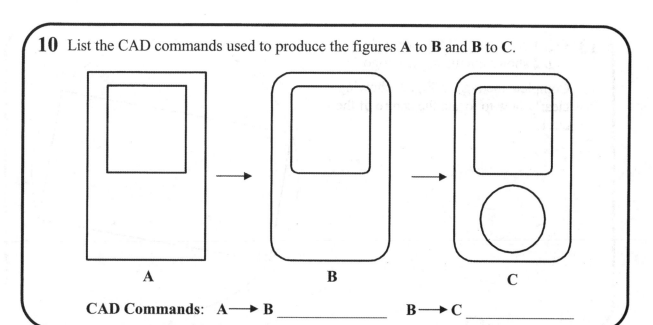

CAD Commands: **A** ⟶ **B** _____ **B** ⟶ **C** _____

11 The diagram shows the outline of a key. Also shown is a 3D graphic of the key. The handgrip is based on a regular hexagon. Complete the regular hexagon.

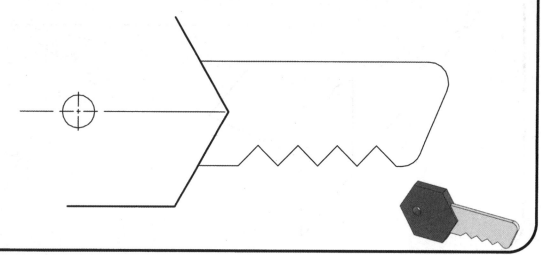

12 Project the **shadow** cast by the letter **H** when the direction of light is parallel to the arrow.

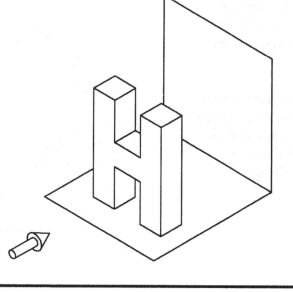

13 **Fig. 1** shows a logo for a card shop.
Fig. 2 shows the incomplete logo.

Complete the logo in **Fig. 2** showing clearly how to locate the centre of the circle.

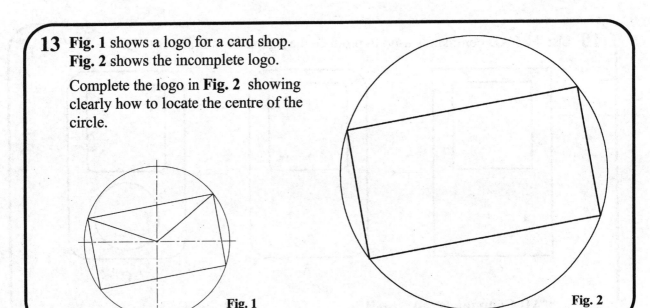

Fig. 1

Fig. 2

14 The figure shows an **incomplete** perspective drawing of a writing unit.
A small 3D graphic of the unit is also shown. **Complete** the perspective drawing.

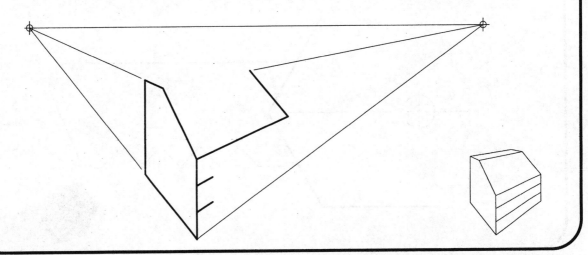

15 The diagram shows the fuel gauge of a car.

Rotate the needle about its centre to show when the fuel tank is half full.

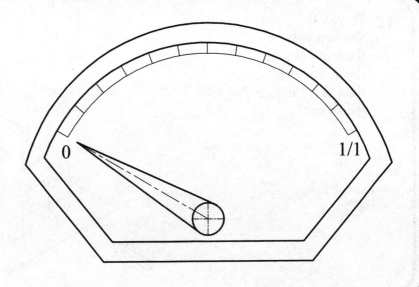

0

1/1

Coimisiún na Scrúduithe Stáit
State Examinations Commission

Junior Certificate Examination, 2010

Technical Graphics
Ordinary Level
Section B
(280 marks)

Monday, 21 June
Morning 9:30 - 12:00

Instructions

(a) Answer **any four** questions. All questions carry equal marks.

(b) The number of the question must be distinctly marked by the side of each answer.

(c) Work on **one side** of the answer paper only.

(d) Write your examination number on each sheet of paper used.

SECTION B. Answer **any four** questions. All questions carry equal marks.

1 The figure shows a design for a mini - DVD player.

Draw:

(a) An elevation in the direction of the arrow **A**.

(b) A plan projected from the elevation.

(c) Insert **any four** dimensions.

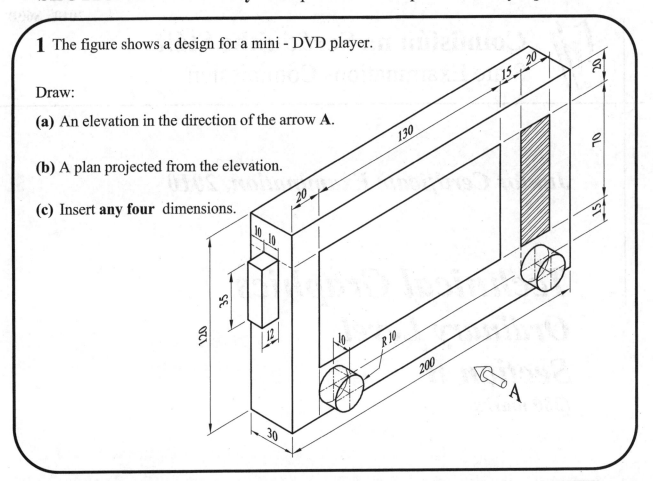

2 The figure shows the design of a logo for a telephone company.

The curve **LMN** is a semi-ellipse as shown.

LN is the major axis and is 140 mm long as shown.

OM is **half** the minor axis and is 40 mm long as shown.

Draw the large circle and then complete the given design.

Show clearly all construction lines.

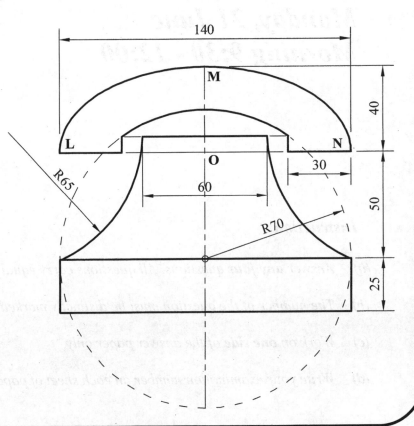

3 The figure shows a design for a scissors holder.

Draw:

(a) An elevation in the direction of arrow **A**.

(b) A plan projected from the elevation.

(c) The complete **surface development** of the scissors holder.

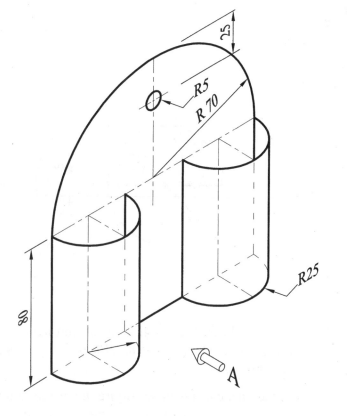

4

240

105

10

The figure shows the elevation and plan of the initials of the **E**nvironmental **P**rotection **A**gency (**EPA**). The grid in elevation is made up of 15 mm squares and the thickness in plan is 10 mm as shown.

Draw **one** of the following views:

(a) An **isometric** view of the initials

or

(b) An **oblique** view of the initials.

Note: The solution must be presented on standard drawing paper.

5

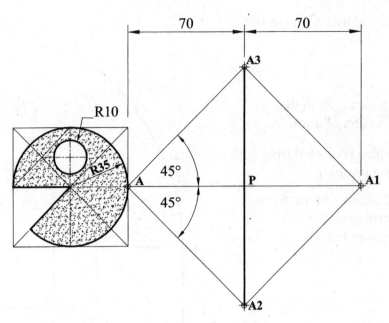

The figure shows the design of a cartoon face.
Draw the given design and then locate the points **A, A1, A2, A3, P** and the line **A2-A3** as shown.

Find the image of the given figure under the following transformations:

(a) From point A to A1 by an **axial symmetry** in the line **A2-A3**
(b) From point A1 to A2 by a **translation**
(c) From point A2 to A3 by a **central symmetry** in the point **P**.

6 The figure shows a design for a safety logo.

Reproduce the given design showing clearly how to find the centres of the circles.

Show all construction lines and points of contact.

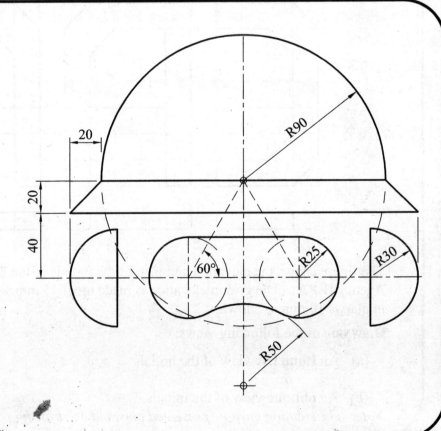